The Creation of the Dáil

A Volume of Essays from the
Thomas Davis Lectures
(GENERAL EDITOR MICHAEL LITTLETON)

EDITED BY BRIAN FARRELL

Published in Association with
RADIO TELEFÍS ÉIREANN

BLACKWATER PRESS

Printed in Ireland at the press of the publishers

© 1994 Blackwater Press,
c/o Folens Publishers,
Broomhill Business Park,
Tallaght,
Dublin 24.

ISBN 0 86121 587 7

Editor
Hilda O'Sullivan

Design & Layout
Edward Callan

Front Cover
Philip Ryan

CONTENTS

ACKNOWLEDGEMENTS

The editor owes a particular debt to:

- Michael Littleton, Features Editor, RTE Radio I, who initiated and produced this series of Thomas Davis lectures broadcast in Spring 1994, for his unstinting support, critical co-operation and friendly professionalism.

- To the authors who compressed so much information and so many insights into broadcast talks and then converted them into readable and elegant essays.

- To John O'Connor for his ready agreement to publish.

- To Hilda O'Sullivan and Susannah Gee for transforming authors' copy to published text with tact, patience and speed.

- And to Geraldine Meyter of the Department of Politics UCD for her invaluable help with this book and throughout many years in UCD.

FOREWORD
BY THE TAOISEACH
ALBERT REYNOLDS

It is very appropriate that, on the 75th Anniversary of the meeting of the First Dáil in the Mansion House on 21 January, 1919, the theme of this year's RTE's Thomas Davis Lectures, which represents public service broadcasting at its best, should be the birth of our democracy.

Professor Brian Farrell has assembled a very distinguished team of contributors to illuminate the key aspects of the First Dáil. This volume explains how democratic institutions were created (or indeed in some cases improvised) that paved the way for long-term political stability, in a way unique among the new independent States that have emerged this century. The political programmes adopted by the First Dáil, its relationship to the army, the county councils and the judicial system are analysed, with insights into the role of the Labour Party and of women.

As always, when analysing a formative period of our history, we can feel a mixture of pride in the remarkable achievements of a generation that showed intense physical and political courage, although faced by formidable obstacles. But we are also rightly conscious of the problems that they were not able to solve. History is always both an inspiration and a spur to action.

November 1994

1

The Parliamentary Road to Independence
Brian Farrell

Brian Farrell is Director-General of the Institute of European Affairs, Dublin and emeritus Professor of Politics, University College Dublin. He has written extensively on many aspects of Irish government and politics and has been contributing editor to three earlier series of Thomas Davis lectures: *The Irish Parliamentary Tradition, Communications and Community in Ireland*, and *De Valera's Constitution and Ours*. Brian Farrell has twice received Jacob's Awards for his work in current affairs broadcasting in RTE and currently presents *Farrell* on RTE 1.

◆◆◆◆◆◆◆◆◆◆

Seventy-five years ago a small group of deputies assembled at the Mansion House in Dublin. They were there to make history and they knew it.[1] The long-pursued dream of an independent Irish parliament was at last to be realised in practice. The first meeting of the First Dáil was to lay the firm constitutional basis of the new Irish state. It would provide, through the troubled infancy of that state, a forum for deliberation and a visible source of legitimate authority. It's unlikely that many of those jostling for position in Dublin that 21 January 1919 were fully aware of that significance.

Outside in Dawson Street they pressed right across the road, climbed the lamp-posts for a glimpse of the arriving leaders. Young Volunteers preserved a good-natured order and a detachment of the Dublin Metropolitan Police managed to keep the trams running. Disappointed visitors who had come all the way to town sought entry in vain.

Those in the know, with official tickets from their TDs, had queued up with invited guests and packed into the Round Room. Space was found for sixty-nine journalists from home and

1

overseas papers; many of them commented on the respectability of those crushed into this technically illegal assembly. The great circular hall of the Mansion House was dense. Contemporary photographs[2] show the ground floor and gallery thronged and, at the back, a line of younger, serious-looking young people, mainly men, some of them priests, gazing at the scene below: a raised rostrum, tables for the clerks, and, before the Speaker's dais, carefully arranged benches offering places for all one hundred and three Irish members returned at the general election of the previous December.

In fact less than a third attended. The roll-call itself became part of the drama. Unionists understandably had ignored the invitation to attend (apart from a formal refusal from Sir Robert Woods, one of the members for Dublin University). When Carson's name was called, there was a ripple of suppressed laughter. But the tension rose as repeatedly the response to a deputy's name was intoned: 'faoi ghlas ag Gallaibh' – imprisoned by the foreigner.

The proceedings were formal, even liturgical. Many of the brief speeches were in Irish; the *Daily Mail* commented next day dryly that 'speaking in a difficult language, and one to which the orator is not born, is a great shortener of political proceedings.'[3] After less than two hours, the Dáil adjourned and next day's papers carried full descriptions but similar patronising judgments. Even the *Manchester Guardian*, generally sympathetic to Irish aspirations, allowed itself to remark of the newly-appointed government: 'one fancies that the Minister of Finance, Home Affairs and all the other dignitaries will be hard put to it to find an outlet for any executive capacity they may possess.' But a young woman in the audience, part of the Wexford contingent, was closer to the reality with her description and comment: 'People waiting asked one another, "Did you ever think you and I would live to see this day?" Never was the past so near, or the present so brave, or the future so full of hope.'[4] Marie Comerford was right. For this first meeting of the

First Dáil was a truly seminal moment for modern Irish political development. By its form, and in its documents, it laid the direction for the new Irish state and, in large measure, for the political process through which it would develop. Far more than the 'episode at Easter' – to use the phrase of Sean MacEntee, himself a participant in both – it marks both the continuance of the mainline Irish political tradition and the true beginning of independence. The brilliance cast by the Easter Rising often obscures the reality that it was the First Dáil which originally established the authentic representative credentials of modern Irish democracy.[5]

For decades it had been evident that the attempt to maintain British rule in Ireland could not be enforced indefinitely. It flew in the face of that potent mix of democratic values and nationalist instinct that was re-shaping the face of Europe from the mid-nineteenth century. It challenged the increasingly liberal views of a modern Britain, struggling itself to be born, to enforce an Act of Union so evidently at odds with majority political opinion in Ireland. At least from the time of Gladstone's conversion to Home Rule onward the question no longer was would Britain withdraw but how and when. On the eve of the Great War the die was finally cast; Home Rule was on the statute book but, for the moment, postponed. So, of course, was the unresolved issue of what to do about what everyone called 'the Ulster Question'.

If many major items remained on the political agenda of early twentieth century Ireland, many others had already been resolved. Long before independence, the shape of a newly emerging modern Irish democratic society was clearly discernible. It was not the product of heroic, militant action; not the stuff of which ballads are made. It cannot be neatly pigeon-holed in a single memorable date.

1916 is the most potent and evocative date in the catalogue of modern Irish political anniversaries. The actors and the circumstances lent themselves to heroic myth-making. A generation of writers, most notably creative writers led by Yeats but including political propagandists and historians, fashioned an interpretive epic that has echoed down the arches of the years. The drama of that short-lived, compact Easter event in Dublin has become inextricably bound up with the accelerated pace of political change so evident in the next half-dozen crowded years in Ireland. The new state that emerged in the 1920s seems such an obvious consequence of that brief rebellion in arms that we are tempted to mistake the Easter Rising for a revolution, marking a new beginning. In reality, it was more of a hiccough in Ireland's uneven yet unmistakable emergence into statehood. In many ways it is more accurate to see 1916 as an episode, and as such a symbol of tremendous force, than tò seek the real roots of the modern Irish state in a more complex set of relations and a far less aggressive and less militant set of political values.

In particular, this more textured historical context is necessary to understand and explain the extraordinary, almost unique, stability so quickly and sturdily achieved by the new Irish state. The scale of that achievement is more readily appreciated by comparing the Irish experience with that of other states emerging into independence in modern times. Their record overall is one of failure; it emphasises the extraordinary difficulty of managing the fragile transition to independence.

Think of what you know about the creation of new state systems in the twentieth century. Within the last few decades, in the aftermath of World War II and the collapse of colonial empires (the Belgian, the Dutch, the French and the British) in Africa and Asia, a plethora of new states have come into being. And what has happened to them? Wherever you look, whether British East or West Africa, the old Indo-China of France or across North Africa, the typical experience of these states has been an inability to establish any kind of social and political order, or a collapse into anarchy and instability, or the political half-life of rule by a military regime. Admittedly in a world of few certainties, at a time when international law and order has problems functioning, in a phase when the gap between the haves and the have-nots is glaringly obvious – in a time like this, how could one expect poor, under developed, inchoate societies to produce stable governmental systems?

But this was not the only great period of twentieth century state creation. World War I also represented a great clash of empires. In defeat, their break-up involved the restoration, creation and inflation of national sovereignty across Central and Eastern Europe. And what has been their story? For different reasons, they also, by and large, found it difficult to establish and maintain any viable liberal-democratic national state. The bloody heritage of that unfinished business of achieving stability is all too evident in the Balkans today.

So, one can say, Ireland is virtually unique among the new nation-states of the twentieth century in creating and maintaining a stable state system in a firmly democratic mode.

That achievement is all the more remarkable when you consider the problems faced by the Irish new state at the very moment of its birth. It confronted not one, but a group of problems, common enough in other emerging states; problems that in other societies have often led to chronic breakdown. Let us just list them briefly

The Irish state was born into a civil war. These internal conflicts, just like wars between states, are destructive and wasteful. They destroy life and property; they squander scarce resources. But much more to the point they destroy the very civic trust that is the secure foundation of a stable democratic society. In all too many cases, new states plunged into such civil strife have not been able to recover. In the Irish case, ten years after that civil war the victors peacefully handed over the reins of government to their opponents following a democratic election.

Secondly the new state had to cope with a disputed border. That raised in a critical way a fundamental question not only about the boundaries of the national territory but about the very legitimacy of the state and its institutions. It also created unstable minorities on both sides of the border. It is a legacy that continues to absorb energies, concerns and resources right down to our own day. Yet, once again, it has not been allowed to become a serious threat to internal stability within the state's own jurisdiction.

A third major challenge for the new Irish state was posed by the presence within its borders of an entrenched minority. The small southern Unionist, mainly Protestant, population was not only historically and religiously distinct but was seen to be economically privileged and a powerful symbol of an alien cultural and political dominance. Such a group has often served as a convenient scapegoat for failed experiments in independence and as a persuasive excuse for the creation of authoritarian regimes. While the question of integrating, and protecting, religious minorities in a pluralist conception of Irish society remains incomplete in the contemporary Republic, it has not been an insurmountable obstacle to the creation of a system which is both representative and stable.

When these three major burdens (of civil war, disputed border and religious difference) are placed against the general background of relative economic underdevelopment, inflated expectations of general prosperity following on the heels of independence, and the lack of any significant executive experience among the new leaders, it could be argued that the challenge of Irish state-building assumes epic proportions. Indeed, it would have been impossible if the immediately preceding years had been quite so 'revolutionary' as has been sometimes suggested. Locating the formative years of the state in a radical political tradition of dissent, rebellion and militancy, culminating in the Easter Rising, makes the achievement of political stability even less explicable.

The explanation has to be found in a different perspective on the Irish historical experience. A perspective that places less emphasis on dramatic public events and on a sentimental and romantic view of physical force. A perspective that identifies the process through which Irish society equipped itself to face the challenge of independence, stability and freedom on a secure basis. That perspective might be termed the parliamentary tradition.

In a Thomas Davis lecture broadcast over thirty years ago, Conor Cruise O'Brien commented that the period from Parnell to Pearse forms 'a sort of crease in time, a featureless valley.... a time in which nothing happens' – except, as he goes on to say, a revolution in land ownership.[6] Certainly if that often misused term 'revolution' is taken to mean fundamental, rapid change then it is not misapplied. The transition to a property-owning democracy inherent in the Wyndham Land Act of 1903 marked a real revolution. It reduced the risk that agrarian violence, agitation and land-grabbing might coincide with political and constitutional demands. It brought to an end the *ancien regime* of landlord rule which had dominated Irish society since the plantations and confiscations of the sixteenth and seventeenth centuries. It removed any justification for government coercion which, in the past, had been used to suppress not only sedition and rebellion but also to subdue the legitimate expression of public opinion. It transformed a potentially revolutionary population of landless peasants into property-owners with a vested interest in the *status quo* domestically. But paradoxically the Wyndham Land Act also meant that a new, populous class of small farmers no longer had any substantial interest in what went on at Westminster.

Land distribution, which has so often proved a disastrously divisive issue for many new states – it has contributed, right down to our own day, to the chronic instability of the Balkans – was already largely settled before the Irish state came into existence.

Moreover, notwithstanding a long history of agrarian outrage and agitation, it was settled by essentially political action and parliamentary statute. The same could be said for other major advances in Irish political development.

For many new states, it is the need to face all their developmental problems in a simultaneous moment that creates an insurmountable burden. Confronted with unresolved internal tensions – economic, racial and religious, saddled with chronic neglect, buffeted by a revolution of rising expectations, they have often been overwhelmed by the sheer scale of the quantum-leap from colonial dependency to self-rule. Many western nations, by comparison, have experienced a more benign and gradual developmental chronology; their problems have been spaced-out over longer time periods; their progress, though sometimes spasmodic, has been more orderly. That has been a major contributor to state stability. Ireland was fortunate to experience this more measured progress towards modernisation.

The systematic exclusion of the Catholic majority from legal rights marked the first threshold to be crossed. It was the Bastille of the *ancien regime*, an outright rejection of popular rights and values. The penal laws were more ramshackle, intermittent and ineffective in practice than the draconian theory dictated. Nevertheless, while they remained on the statute book, no progress was possible; even unused, they were a powerful symbol of dominance by a feudal oligarchy. What finally, and irrevocably, breached that Bastille was the election of O'Connell to Westminster and the subsequent passage of the Catholic Emancipation Act of 1829. That statute effectively defused the most immediately explosive issues of church-state relations.

Similarly, it was a series of Westminster laws, supported and pressed by Irish members, that created a process leading inexorably to universal adult suffrage. From the great Reform Bill of 1832, through a variety of later measures dealing with the extension of the franchise, the elimination of corrupt practices, and the introduction of the secret ballot, Britain created for itself the electoral framework within which to achieve democratically accountable government. Ireland, as part of the Union, shared in that widening of political power.

Gradually many of the harsh and intractable problems that oppress newly emerging states were resolved. By the turn of the century, there was a school system that (whatever its lack of opportunity at second and third level) supplied a basic literacy for the whole population. A transport and communication network was spread across the country. Trade unions were established and, however reluctantly, accepted. There was a modern, stable, administrative machine increasingly open (at least at lower and middle level) to local recruitment. Indeed, the whole apparatus of the state and the necessary networks of civic culture were securely in place long before independence.

So, too, were the political leaders due to inherit this infant polity. The Irish Parliamentary party were clearly established as heirs apparent to a modern Ireland they had done so much to create. Even before Home Rule, they were recognised as power-brokers, consulted over senior appointments and apparently securely placed to take possession of the new Ireland as it gained legislative independence.

Set beside these serried ranks of established parliamentarians, the claims of more advanced nationalists to speak for that new Ireland seemed peripheral, even eccentric. The growth of a cultural nationalism powerfully propelled by movements and organisations as diverse as the GAA, the Gaelic League and the Irish Literary Revival could be accommodated, where it could not be ignored. Even more modern ideas about workers rights and women's suffrage need not be mentioned. Problems of poverty, whether in rural Ireland or urban slums, were matters of charity rather than subjects for public policy. The leaders of the Irish

Parliamentary party, despite the disastrous and long-term bickering of the Parnellite split and the ill-considered recruiting campaign that later split the Volunteers, were recognised as the most likely recipients of any transfer of power after Home Rule.

The fact that this did not happen owes less to the Easter Rising than to the men and women who took over the leadership of the Irish nation in the years immediately afterwards. The First Dáil was at once their opportunity and their monument. In this volume of essays based on the Thomas Davis lectures broadcast in 1994 we will examine how those critical transitional years leading to legislative independence were managed.

The volume describes the circumstances of the 1918 General Election – the last all-Ireland election to the Westminster Parliament held in Ireland. Also, of course, the first election held under a system of adult male suffrage and a contest that revealed in the starkest terms yet the depth of division between the North-East and the rest of Ireland. This is the subject of John Coakley's essay.

In a separate essay, Professor Tom Garvin analyses the nature and sources of the new political elite that snatched the reins of leadership from the old Parliamentary party. Professor Maryann Valiulis traces the expectations of independence harboured by the women who played such an active part in its realisation and the disappointment of those hopes as the new state settled down.

A discussion of the fundamental documents formally adopted by the First Dáil, including its constitution and the 'Democratic Programme', is followed by three essays dealing with central aspects of the Dáil's effort to establish, in Arthur Griffith's words, 'a polity within a polity'. Mary Kotsonouris, author of a newly published book on the Dáil courts, deals with one of the most ambitious and effective efforts to create an alternative system of justice – the creation of an integrated organisation of people's courts and the subsequent retreat from this brave enterprise. Dr Eunan O'Halpin examines the complex relationship between the

Dáil and its armed forces; issues of overlapping civil and military authority, always problematic, become critical in a phase of insurgency and, in the Irish case, form the background to the civil war. Then Dr Mary Daly addresses the work of the one department of state, established by the First Dáil, which is acknowledged to have achieved a degree of success – the Local Government department headed by W.T. Cosgrave.

Finally, to round off this volume marking the 75th anniversary of the First Dáil, Professor Joe Lee places this first independent Irish parliament of the twentieth century in the broader context of Irish historical and political development.

Of course, none of these developments could have taken place without a sufficiently mature and organised political vehicle to carry forward the forces of change in early twentieth-century Ireland. The First Dáil did not spring forth as some newly invented and entirely novel solution to the so-called 'Irish problem'. It was, as I have already suggested, the late manifestation of an already established, effective and popular parliamentary tradition.

In Ireland, as elsewhere, the growth of representative government has often been fractured. It has been frequently ineffective in its application, often tardy, almost always incomplete in its range. Parliaments in the past, as in the present, have failed to identify problems in time, failed to cope with pressing needs, failed to provide for future demands. Yet the representative mode, and its concurrent commitment to free and competitive elections has never been abandoned by the majority of the Irish people. Whether at home or among the Irish emigrant communities in Britain, North America and Australia, the Irish have, almost instinctively, embraced political organisation, created and run parties, sought power on the basis of a popular mandate.

To say this is not to indulge is some historical revisionism for its own sake. Still less is it to attempt a dismissive reduction of the powerful influence of the 1916 Rising on the men and women of the generation that witnessed, participated in, and inherited the aftermath of that dramatic event. Many of those most actively involved (Michael Collins is an outstanding example) were themselves critical of the tactics adopted. Others (notably Eoin MacNeill) were dubious of the morality of armed rebellion. All were influenced by the immediate event and by a longer political tradition.

For any understanding of the process by which Ireland emerged into independent statehood – and achieved such remarkable political stability – it is necessary to recover, know and appreciate more fully the detailed developments that occurred in the years immediately after the Rising. A great political experiment was attempted. It involved a massive organisational effort, an extraordinary mobilisation and focussing of public opinion. That was the achievement of those who built on the ashes of that failure at Easter.

In the re-shaping of Irish political destinies in the middle of a great war and after the failure of the Easter Rising, the newly emerging political elite looked for an early electoral opportunity to claim leadership of the Irish people. They found it in a series of bye-elections in 1917 and 1918 and, in the process, created a new political party with an old name – Sinn Féin. The evolution of that party, from the ginger-group founded by Arthur Griffith through to a nationwide organisation that swept into power with an overwhelming majority in the general election of 1918 and created the First Dáil, is the subject of the next essay.

Notes

1. Some of this chapter is based on Brian Farrell, '*A Note on the Dáil Constitution, 1919*', in *Irish Jurist*, IV, I, Summer 1969, which gives detailed references.

2. See C.B.S., *The Irish Uprising 1919-1922*, distributed by Macmillan 1966, pp.69-71.

3. This and subsequent quotation from the *Manchester Guardian* in Robert Kee, *The Green Flag*, Delacorte Press, New York 1972, pp. 630-1.

4. Marie Comerford, *The First Dáil*, Joe Clark publisher, Dublin 1969.

5. This argument is developed further in Brian Farrell, *The Founding of Dáil Éireann: parliament and nation-building*, Gill and Macmillan, Dublin 1971 and his edited volume *The Irish Parliamentary Tradition*, Gill and Macmillan, Dublin 1974.

6. Conor Cruise O'Brien, *1891-1916* in Conor Cruise O'Brien, ed., *The Shaping of Modern Ireland*, Routledge and Kegan Paul, London 1960, p.13.

2

Sinn Féin from Dual Monarchy to the First Dáil

Michael Laffan

Michael Laffan is a lecturer in the Department of Modern Irish History in University College Dublin. He is the author of *The Partition of Ireland, 1911-1925* and of various articles on Irish history, and has edited *The Burden of German History, 1919-1945*. He is at present working on a study of the Sinn Féin party between 1916 and 1923.

♦♦♦♦♦♦♦♦♦♦

In two quite different respects the meeting of the First Dáil in January 1919 was an act of great symbolic importance. Not only did it inaugurate the democratic and constitutional history of independent Ireland, but it also represented a synthesis of two different traditions within Irish nationalism.

At one level it continued the momentum of Easter Week. The republic which Pearse had proclaimed on the steps of the General Post Office, and which the rebels had defended in arms for the next six days, was now solemnly re-proclaimed in the Mansion House by a democratically-elected Irish parliament. The Dáil thereby established continuity with the recent past and conferred retrospective legitimacy on the 1916 Rising.

At another level this meeting of the Dáil was the climax of policies which Arthur Griffith had advocated for two decades; it implemented his belief that Irish MPs should abstain from Westminster; that they should reconstitute themselves as an independent Irish parliament in Dublin; and that, in so far as circumstances allowed, they should proceed to administer Ireland as if British rule and the crown forces did not exist. The convening of an independent parliament was the natural, logical culmination of a political movement and a political process which went back to the early years of the century.

But the First Dáil can be seen as a synthesis in a quite different sense. It was also the result of a recent interaction between the military and the political traditions within Irish nationalism. It was the product of co-operation between soldiers (the Irish Volunteers) and politicians (Griffith's Sinn Féin party and others) which already existed before the Dáil met; and this co-operation was a central part of the process which led to the creation of an independent Irish parliament.

The party which won the 1918 general election, and whose elected members then proceeded to constitute the Dáil, was in many respects the creation of Arthur Griffith. He was an improbable politician, cranky, taciturn and at times almost self-effacing, a man who preferred to influence others rather than achieve power himself. He was inclined to dislike and distrust much political activity. He was a gifted journalist, happiest with a pen in his hand, polishing phrases, outlining policies, compiling statistics, and denouncing his numerous enemies in the columns of his various newspapers.[1]

Griffith believed that Ireland should seek to establish a dual monarchy in which the country would be fully independent and would share only a common king with Great Britain. His model for future Anglo-Irish relations was the Habsburg empire, in which Franz Joseph was both emperor of Austria and king of Hungary but in which the two countries had separate parliaments and governments. This was a parallel which he advocated in his booklet, *The Resurrection of Hungary,* and in numerous articles, pamphlets and speeches.

He designed his scheme in the hope that he would be able to effect a compromise which would be acceptable to three different elements: the British government, Irish republicans, and the moderate majority of Irish nationalists. Until after the Easter

Rising, none of these groups was prepared to accept his ideas. During the early years of the twentieth century he was involved in various committees and societies, and eventually he formed his own organisation, the National Council. This always remained more of a lobby or a pressure group than a political party, and rather than supplant the Irish Parliamentary Party Griffith would have preferred to convert it to his views. He named his newspaper *Sinn Féin*, a term which was current and fashionable at the time.

The early, pre-1916 Sinn Féin has always been associated with Griffith, but ironically he was not a member when the first party of that name was founded in 1907 by other, more radical figures. Some of them objected to his moderate opinions, and in particular they were unimpressed by his plans for reviving Grattan's parliament and for reconstituting its King, Lords and Commons of Ireland. However he was soon able to take over this Sinn Féin party, and he merged it with his own National Council so that the new entity reflected his moderate and 'monarchist' beliefs. He was helped by the fact that his arguments converted one of the Redmondite Home Rule MPs, Charles Dolan of North Leitrim, and for a while it seemed as if Griffith's programme might pose a serious challenge to the Parliamentary Party. Dolan resigned his seat and then ran for re-election as a Sinn Féiner with the programme of abstaining from parliament. The result was a long, protracted by-election campaign, spread over many months; in the end he lost to the Home Rule candidate by a margin of three to one. This was the only parliamentary seat which the Sinn Féin party ever contested until after the Easter Rising.

Before the First World War Redmond's Home Rule party represented the vast majority of Irish nationalists, and Griffith's Sinn Féin was not a significant force in Irish public life. It never had more than 130 branches, and most of these soon faded away. Republicans (even members of the IRB) joined it in the early days, but after a while they lost interest and turned their energies elsewhere. Yet even though Griffith's party was discredited and almost forgotten, he himself remained an influential figure and his newspapers continued to be widely read. The name 'Sinn Féin' remained in general use, and in some cases it was attached to groups whose members had little sympathy with Griffith or with his enthusiasm for Grattan's Parliament and the Habsburg Empire.

The British political crisis of 1909-11 re-opened the Home Rule question, and in the course of the next few years the Ulster unionists under Edward Carson posed a different and more formidable challenge to the moderate nationalist cause. Their establishment of a private army undermined Redmond and mocked his insistence that Irish nationalists should operate by the rules of the House of Commons.[2] The unionists also inspired radical nationalists to follow their example and to found a rival army, the Irish Volunteers. From the very beginning this force was infiltrated by the IRB, and it was a section of the Volunteers (assisted by Connolly's Citizen Army) which staged the Easter Rising.

The 1916 rebels struck a blow at what they regarded as the iniquity of British rule and the inadequacy of Home Rule; but in some respects their insurrection might also seem to have been an indirect attack on Griffith and what he represented. After all, his aims were far less extreme than the republic which was proclaimed in Easter Week, and he believed in using peaceful means to achieve them. Despite this he was arrested in its aftermath; he had not been involved in the fighting, but the British felt – quite rightly – that he had influenced many of those who were. And in the course of the next few months the name 'Sinn Féin', already ascribed to the Volunteers, now became attached to the Rising as well.

When Griffith was released from jail at Christmas 1916 he was able to avail of the changes in public opinion which had been precipitated by the Rising, by the executions and the widespread arrests which followed it, and also by the humiliation of the

Parliamentary Party as it made yet another unsuccessful attempt to achieve Home Rule. His moribund Sinn Féin had achieved little during the months of his imprisonment, but it could now begin to exploit the newly-favourable circumstances.

The turning point came a few weeks later with the North Roscommon by-election in February 1917. Headed by a local curate, Fr Michael O'Flanagan, a group of radical nationalists decided to challenge the Parliamentary Party. Their candidate was Count Plunkett, an elderly scholar who had little claim to prominence except as the father of a signatory of the Easter Week proclamation. A miscellaneous band of dissidents gathered in Roscommon to canvass on his behalf. These included Griffith and some of his followers from the old Sinn Féin party, and also members of the newly-formed Irish Nation League, consisting of Home Rulers who had become disillusioned with Redmond and his methods.

Perhaps the most important feature of the campaign is that Plunkett's varied supporters included many Irish Volunteers. Former rebels such as Michael Collins were deeply suspicious of politicians. Their training and experience had led them to regard political activity with distaste; they associated it with the Parliamentary Party, and with compromise, disappointment and frustration. Many saw themselves as an elite which represented the soul, or heart, or will of the Irish nation, and they despised the vast majority of their contemporaries as feeble and unimaginative, as unworthy heirs to the heroic tradition of Irish insurrection. They believed that only violence would shock the inert masses into rediscovering their true identity, and few if any of them had contemplated using peaceful, political measures to bring about a national regeneration.

Nonetheless, many of the Volunteers realised that there was little chance of their being able to resume their fight against the British in the foreseeable future. As a second-best they were prepared to confront a lesser enemy, the Redmondites; and they realised (often only slowly and with great reluctance) that they could do this only by beating the experienced politicians at their own electoral game. The Volunteers were able to apply their military discipline to an unfamiliar and unexpected sort of campaign, and, perhaps to their own surprise, they proved to be remarkably successful in their new role.

These different elements which supported Plunkett in North Roscommon were not yet a party and they had no positive programme; they were a coalition of different interests and individuals. At this stage they could only agree in their common dislike of the British Government and of the Home Rule movement. But this one supreme bond of a common enemy transcended all their differences, and they co-operated harmoniously together as they fought through the snowstorms which dominated the campaign. Plunkett won by a large majority, the Redmondites' morale was badly shaken (so much so that Redmond even contemplated withdrawing from public life[3]) and the various radical groups were encouraged to continue working together.

These 'advanced nationalists' were normally called Sinn Féiners, even though many of them were Volunteers who were wary of Griffith's party and who rejected his idea of a dual monarchy. Many of them remained blindly loyal to their ideal of the republic which had been proclaimed during the Easter Rising. One of those most critical of Griffith at this time was his future ally Collins, who in 1917 was still a radical and inflexible republican; his ability to compromise was acquired only in later years. During the course of the next few months the different factions quarrelled among themselves, and at one stage Count Plunkett even tried to found his own political organisation in opposition to Griffith's Sinn Féin. But these disputes did not prevent them from combining in their common fight against the Redmondites.

Griffith presided over the revival of his party, and he was able to build on and consolidate the change of opinion which had followed the rising. He helped politicise the radicalisation of Irish nationalist opinion. Sinn Féin was the mood, or fashion, or trend, of 1917, and hundreds of new branches were formed throughout the country. One Sinn Féin club would establish another in a neighbouring village or parish, and for a time the party seemed to spread in geometric progression. Speakers travelled from meeting to meeting, propaganda was produced and distributed, and a party headquarters functioned busily in Dublin. Sinn Féin exuded a contagious energy and vitality, and observers drew parallels with the excitement which had characterised the Parnellite movement in the 1880s. For many people, involvement in the party's activities was an antidote to the monotony of daily life. By the end of the year Sinn Féin was organised and self- confident, and its membership totalled about 150,000; zealous enthusiasts were accompanied by others who were more cautious, conservative and opportunistic.

In terms of its mass membership, its energy, its radicalism, and its military backbone, Sinn Féin in 1917 was a new party and not merely a continuation of Griffith's earlier organisation. Nonetheless his pre-Rising party was able to make a significant contribution to the new mass movement, providing it with a structure, with most (although not all) of its policies, and with politically-experienced leaders.

One of the most remarkable aspects of this development was that the majority of these party members were recent converts to the ideas of Sinn Féin – to policies such as abstention from Westminster and the establishment of an independent national parliament. Until only a year or two earlier, most of those who now cheered and canvassed for Sinn Féin had been followers of Redmond and Home Rule. This rapid conversion of an already-politicised electorate ensured that many of the new recruits brought into the new party their democratic assumptions and their old skills or habits; in this indirect manner the Parliamentary Party

CREATION OF THE DÁIL

influenced its successful rival.[4] Here, too, there was a form of synthesis. Sinn Féin's leadership was influenced by romantic republicanism, the linguistic nationalism of the Irish-Ireland movement, and by Griffith's more down-to-earth concern with economic independence, while the mass of the new party members were accustomed to the methods, the imagery and the limited objectives of the Parliamentary Party. Each influenced the other. As a result the new party was broadly-based and comprehensive, and its rank and file were less extreme in their opinions than were many of the leaders or most of the soldiers. Radical nationalists acquired a mass following which they had lacked before the Rising, but they had to pay a price: the movement in general, and some of its leaders in particular, were reined back by the people's moderation.

North Roscommon was only the first of several by-elections fought by the new movement. The next challenge came in South Longford, where the Sinn Féin movement put forward as its candidate one of the imprisoned Easter rebels, Joe McGuinness. This was a sign of the separatists' confidence that public opinion had moved in their direction, and that they believed voters were now prepared to endorse the memory or the image of the Rising. The campaign was closely fought, and the Redmondites were beaten by a mere 37 votes. It is possible that McGuinness was saved from defeat by the intervention of one man. On the eve of the election the Catholic archbishop of Dublin, William Walsh, made a carefully timed attack on partition and declared that 'the country is practically sold'. This was widely seen and portrayed as a reference to the Parliamentary Party, and his remarks were circulated by Sinn Féiners on election day.

McGuinness had been reluctant to allow his name go forward, and in this he was supported by Eamon de Valera and by others among the Easter rebels who still remained in prison. They feared that to lose the election would be seen as a repudiation of the

Rising; that as de Valera put it, 'his defeat would mean our defeat – the irretrievable ruin of all our comrades died for and all that their death has gained'. But, locked up in an English jail, they were unable to appreciate the extent to which Irish attitudes and circumstances had changed in the year since their rebellion.

Shortly afterwards the different elements in what one could call loosely the Sinn Féin movement combined to form a unified Sinn Féin party. As an interim measure the leaders agreed that Griffith would remain president and that the party's objective would remain that of a dual monarchy; however, it was decided that questions of leadership and policy would be reassessed at a party convention to be held in the autumn. This merger represented an uneasy coalition of republicans and moderates.

A few weeks later the remaining prisoners were released from jail, and within days they were thrown into the third by-election campaign of the year. De Valera was chosen as the candidate to contest the parliamentary vacancy in East Clare – a seat formerly held by Redmond's brother who had been killed fighting in the First World War. De Valera was also co-opted to the executive of Sinn Féin. Until then he had had no connection with any political party; like many others at the time, like men such as Patrick Pearse and Eoin MacNeill, he had moved directly from cultural to military nationalism. He was a late convert to politics, although he made up for lost time and soon learned the tricks of the trade.

The fact that the internal quarrels between Griffith and Plunkett had ended shortly before, and that the new party clearly represented a substantial body of Irish nationalist opinion (possibly already a majority) made it easier for suspicious soldiers to engage in political activity. Volunteers were active throughout the campaign, and in some cases they took over police duties from the RIC. (Their influence did not always reinforce law and order; on election day the roads to some polling stations were blocked by cars, and voters were asked about their intentions before being allowed to proceed.[5]) As one sign of the Sinn Féiners' confidence, de Valera and others made speeches in which they demanded a republic; it was clear that for many in the Irish Volunteers, Griffith's ideas of a dual monarchy were quite inadequate and could now be repudiated. The outcome of East Clare was never in doubt; the Home Rulers were routed, and de Valera won over two thirds of the vote. Soon afterwards, almost as a postscript, W T Cosgrave was elected for Kilkenny City.

These four by-elections of 1917 were of enormous importance. Already by the beginning of the year many Irish nationalists had become disillusioned with the Home Rule cause and party, but they could see no realistic alternative, they were disorganised, and they had no leadership, policy, or sense of direction. Then, after a private initiative in North Roscommon had broken the deadlock, radical nationalists simply turned up in the constituency and acquired the habit of working together. This experience proved contagious, and one success led to another. One pamphlet printed for the Clare election boasted that Sinn Féin was an invincible force 'and its effects follow each other with regularity and rapidity'.[6] The by-elections generated enthusiasm and publicity – and they imposed unity on what was still a fractious coalition of different interests and traditions. The need to fight the Redmondites helped prevent the new movement from falling apart, and also helped transform it from a movement to a political party. The impact of these local victories spread throughout the whole country, and by the end of the year there was a Sinn Féin branch in virtually every parish in nationalist Ireland.

The final stage in the party's revival came with the convention held in October 1917 at which over a thousand branches were represented. As the result of a prior agreement between the two men de Valera replaced Griffith as president, and at the same time the party also finally abandoned the ideas of Grattan's Parliament and its King, Lords and Commons of Ireland. Griffith's policy of a dual monarchy linking Ireland with Britain was buried – little more than a year before the final collapse of the Austro-Hungarian monarchy which had been his inspiration. Instead, the new Sinn Féin committed itself unambiguously to the aim of an Irish republic; it would complete the work begun by the rebels of Easter Week. Some enthusiasts interpreted the word 'republic' in a literal sense, but, as later events would prove, for many others it was no more than a synonym for independence.

This adherence to a republic was natural in the circumstances of the time, yet it can be seen as a rare example of the party allowing ideology to triumph over practical considerations; of the radical Volunteers overcoming the more cautious politicians. It was a fateful decision – although its full significance would not become apparent for another four years, until the Treaty provoked a split between the moderates and the extremist republicans who had coalesced in October 1917. In December 1921 Griffith's aim of a dual monarchy would be revived and incorporated in the Anglo-Irish Treaty, although in a somewhat different form. Then some of the leading figures in the Sinn Féin movement (along with most of the Volunteers) would either refuse to accept any compromise, or else would reject the only compromise which was on offer. The two traditions which had been subsumed in one united movement in the course of 1917 would be wrenched apart, and the natural fault-line between them would be revealed once more. But in the euphoria of unity and victory, few of those present in the Mansion House at the party's convention in October 1917 would have looked ahead with such foreboding.

Even in the short run, however, the new 'republicanised' Sinn Féin encountered serious problems. In the first months of 1918 the party suffered a number of reverses, and it lost three by-elections in succession, in South Armagh, Waterford City and East Tyrone. Many people wondered whether the tide might have turned against Sinn Féin, and some Home Rulers felt able to indulge in a short-lived bout of optimism, but Griffith and others argued that all three constituencies were unrepresentative of nationalist opinion. This is exactly what party spokesmen would say in such circumstances, and some observers were understandably sceptical. But it was probably true. Waterford was a special case; it had been Redmond's own seat, and now after his death it was contested by his son. The Parliamentary Party could call on a sympathy vote, as well as on a tradition of loyalty to the Redmond family.

The other two defeats took place in Ulster, where the Home Rule party was stronger than elsewhere. There was a simple reason for this regional variation. Throughout most of the country the Parliamentary Party had encountered few or no serious challenges since the early 1890s, and as a result it became flabby, complacent, and vulnerable. But in Ulster, where Home Rulers had always faced formidable opposition from their Unionist rivals, they were kept alert, remained highly efficient, and were forced to be responsive to the voters' needs and wishes. Only in the northeast were they able to resist the Sinn Féin onslaught. In the general election at the end of the year the pattern would be repeated, and the Parliamentary Party was once again able to perform better in Ulster than in southern constituencies.

Sinn Féin's fortunes were restored by the conscription crisis in the spring of 1918. Military service had been enforced in Britain for more than two years, and there were natural fears that it would be extended to Ireland as well. In the 1917 by-elections both sides had claimed credit for averting the threat. Finally in the spring of 1918, faced with the prospect of military defeat as the Germans broke through the allied positions on the Western Front, Lloyd George's cabinet and the House of Commons decided at last to impose conscription on Ireland. The British ignored sound advice to the contrary which they received from Carson and others who were familiar with the realities of Irish life.

The Parliamentary Party MPs opposed the measure, and when they were outvoted by British members they returned to Ireland to carry on the fight at home. By doing this, of course, they put into effect the ideas which Griffith had advocated for the past twenty years: that Irish representatives should withdraw from Westminster and should meet instead in Dublin. But they did so reluctantly, and in circumstances which represented a humiliating defeat for their own policies.

Sinn Féin and the Volunteers were more appropriate leaders of Irish nationalist opinion as it united against the Military Service Act. Radical measures were called for, and it seemed only natural that the initiative should be taken by radical men. Sinn Féin led the civilian opposition, and as the Volunteers prepared for another rebellion they were strengthened by the confidence that this time, in contrast to 1916, they would have the mass of the people behind them. The *Irish Independent* warned that the Easter Rising would be seen as no more than a trifling incident in comparison with violence to come if conscription were to be imposed on the country.[7] Sinn Féin became the *de facto* leader of a nationalist coalition, and in the eyes of many cautious nationalists it acquired a new degree of respectability. This was enhanced by the co-operation between the nationalist leaders and the Catholic hierarchy which characterised the anti-conscription campaign. Faced with unanimous opposition outside unionist north-east Ulster the British government backed down, and conscription was postponed indefinitely. Shortly afterwards, in what seemed like an act of spite or revenge, the Sinn Féin leaders were arrested.

De Valera, Griffith and many other prominent members of the party spent most of the next year in jail, but senior military figures such as Collins, Brugha and Mulcahy remained at liberty. The arrests of May 1918 began a process which would reach its climax only in the course of the next few years: the gradual overshadowing of the political wing of the republican movement by its military counterpart. In the short run, however, the party's fortunes were revived by the conscription crisis and the repression which followed it. It was able to point out that only Sinn Féiners had been arrested, while Home Rulers were left free; obviously the British government did not regard them as a serious threat to its measures. John Dillon, the new leader of the Parliamentary Party, felt that the government had deliberately undermined him and his colleagues by ignoring them and martyring only their enemies. Republicans could claim, with a considerable degree of justification, that it was they who had saved nationalist Ireland from conscription.

Sinn Féin's popularity was confirmed by the final by-election of the year, in East Cavan. There, with the imprisoned Arthur Griffith as its candidate, it defeated the Parliamentary Party after a long campaign and by a decisive margin. For the next six months Sinn Féiners were able to remind the population of their role in averting the conscription menace; the British government refused to abandon the measure, and threatened to introduce compulsory military service at some stage in the future. The result was predictable: fear and tension were maintained until the very end of the war in November 1918, and they were accompanied by a feeling of gratitude to Sinn Féin and the Volunteers who were seen as having saved the young men of Ireland from the slaughter of the battlefields in France.

By now Sinn Féin was undoubtedly the dominant force in nationalist Ireland. It had proved itself a disciplined and successful party, it had converted and organised public opinion, and it had humiliated its Home Rule rival. But it could not begin to implement other aspects of its programme until it was given the opportunity to form an independent Irish parliament and government. And for that the party was obliged to wait until the general elections which were held after the end of the war. Then, in December 1918, Sinn Féin was able to bring to a triumphant climax its achievements of the previous two years.

Notes

1.   Virginia Glandon, *Arthur Griffith and the Advanced-Nationalist Press in Ireland, 1900-1922* (New York, 1985), pp 41-57

2.   Alvin Jackson, *Sir Edward Carson* (Dublin, 1993), pp 30-41; Michael Laffan, *The Partition of Ireland, 1911-1925* (Dublin, 1983), pp 29-30

3.   F.S.L. Lyons, *John Dillon* (London, 1968), p. 411

4.   David Fitzpatrick, *Politics and Irish Life: Provincial Experience of War and Revolution* (Dublin, 1977), pp 118, 137-8

5.   *Saturday Record*, 14 July 1917

6.   *Sinn Féin Releases the Prisoners* (pamphlet, 1917)

7.   *Irish Independent*, 13 April 1918

3
The Election that made the First Dáil
John Coakley

John Coakley is Lecturer in Politics in University College Dublin, and Secretary General of the International Political Science Association. He has published extensively on nationalism, ethnic conflict and Irish politics, has edited *The Social Origins of Nationalist Movements* (London 1992) and *The Territorial Management of Ethnic Conflict* (London 1993) and has coedited *Politics in the Republic of Ireland* (2nd ed, Dublin 1993).

◆◆◆◆◆◆◆◆◆◆

When the Irish people went to the polls at the general election of December 1918, it is unlikely that they realised the enormous consequences that would follow from their votes. Even the most committed Sinn Féin supporters could scarcely believe the results. As one of them put it:

'To those of us who had been in Sinn Féin from the beginning, it was difficult to realise that the election of 1918 was not a dream. ... that in our lifetime we would see the whole of Ireland committed – even the business men and the strong farmers and clerics – committed to the policy of Sinn Féin on a separatist basis, was never seriously entertained by anybody.'[1]

Without a doubt, the 1918 general election was one of the greatest electoral landslides in western Europe in the twentieth century. We know from the study of voting behaviour that parties tend to be stable in their support, and that elections are normally unsurprising in their results. Once a party has developed an extensive organisation and set down firm roots among the voters, it becomes difficult to dislodge. Its loyal core of supporters will abandon the party only in the most extreme circumstances.[2]

The Irish Nationalist Party appeared to be in just such a fortunate position. Founded by Isaac Butt in the 1870s and led to a central role on the political stage by Charles Stewart Parnell in the 1880s, the party had been the dominant force in Irish political life for more than 30 years. Although the party had suffered from internal divisions that at times were intense, Nationalist MPs normally held between 80 and 85 of Ireland's 103 seats in the House of Commons at Westminster.[3] The party's electoral machine, the United Irish League, had a network of about one thousand branches spread throughout the country.

The Nationalist party lost six seats to the new, vibrant Sinn Féin movement in by-elections during 1917 and 1918. It nevertheless approached the 1918 general election as a powerful party. The handful of Sinn Féin MPs appeared insignificant alongside the 77 Nationalist MPs. Yet the result of the election completely reversed this relationship: Sinn Féin MPs were returned to 73 seats, while the Nationalists' share dwindled to six.[4]

The scale of the Sinn Féin victory over the Nationalists will become clear if we consider the results in greater detail (see a summary of the results in Appendix I). The most prominent Nationalist candidate, the party leader, John Dillon, was defeated by a two-to-one majority by Eamon de Valera in Mayo East, a constituency he had held for 33 years. In fact, only two of the six surviving Nationalist MPs, Joseph Devlin in Belfast and Captain William Redmond in Waterford, had fought off the Sinn Féin challenge. The other four, all in Ulster constituencies, had won thanks to an election pact between Sinn Féin and the Nationalist Party.

This pact, under whose terms the Catholic primate, Cardinal Logue, had ultimately been given the role of arbitrator, had divided eight Ulster constituencies between Sinn Féin and the Nationalists, allocating four to each. These constituencies were ones where the non-unionist majority was small and where there was a good chance that competition between the Nationalists and Sinn Féin would hand the seats to the Unionists. Incidentally, although Sinn Féin delivered on its commitment and ensured that the Nationalists won their four seats, the Nationalists kept their side of the bargain in only three constituencies. In the fourth, Down East, they put forward a candidate who attracted sufficient support away from Sinn Féin to allow the Unionist to win (see Appendix I). A Unionist candidate, Sir Maurice Dockrell, won in the Dublin constituency of Rathmines, but the Unionist vote here was so solid that no anti-unionist pact could have overturned it.

Although critics of Sinn Féin pointed out that the party had won only 47 per cent of the total votes cast at this election, this figure, though accurate, is a serious understatement of the party's real electoral strength. The fact was that in a very large number of constituencies, 25 in all, Sinn Féin's position was so strong that no candidate of any other party was prepared to go forward, and the Sinn Féin candidate was elected without a contest. This was the case throughout the seven Cork county constituencies, the four Kerry constituencies and the two Clare constituencies, for instance. If we make allowance for the probable level of Sinn Féin strength in these constituencies, then we can estimate that its overall support throughout the island was at least 51 per cent, and was probably rather more than this (see Appendix I).

Of course, the Sinn Féin landslide was even more pronounced in the 26 counties that now constitute the Republic of Ireland. There, Sinn Féin won 69 out of a total of 72 territorial seats. Its support in contested constituencies amounted to 65 per cent of the total vote. The results in those constituencies where it did best in a straight fight with the Nationalist Party speak for themselves. For example, Sinn Féin won 87 percent of the vote in Mayo West, 86 percent in Galway South, 85 per cent in Leitrim and 82 per cent in each of the constituencies of Sligo South, Kildare South, Kilkenny South and Wicklow West. It is true that the Nationalist party vote held up well in some constituencies and that in others it actually increased numerically (though not as a percentage). But overall, it was unable to win sufficient support from new voters to avoid a humiliating defeat.

The stunning upset of 1918 had elements in common with two well-known recent electoral revolutions. The first is the election in South Africa on 26-28 April 1994 that swept the African National Congress (ANC) to victory, largely as a consequence of a fundamental change in the electoral franchise (though domestic political circumstances were also of great significance). With the abolition of a racist franchise and the introduction of universal suffrage, the numbers entitled to vote increased from five to 22 million, and the ANC, previously unrepresented in parliament, was swept to victory with 65 per cent of the vote.

The second example is the election in Italy on 26-27 March 1994 that brought an end to a long period of continuous government by the same parties, largely as a consequence of citizen dissatisfaction with the political complacency and corruption of the old elite (though change in the electoral rules also played a role). More than 58 per cent of the vote went to entirely 'new' parties (even if some of them amounted to little more than a repackaging of older parties), while most of the remainder was divided between parties that were no more than a few years old (such as the reconstituted former communists, the greens and the Northern League).

While it would be misleading to draw close parallels between these elections and the one that took place in Ireland three quarters of a century earlier, they draw attention respectively to two sets of forces that appear to have influenced the outcome in 1918: first, democratisation of the electoral law; and, second, competition between new and established parties in circumstances of political upheaval.

The Irish electoral system had remained almost unchanged since the mid-1880s. At that time, the country had been divided into 100 territorial constituencies. With the exception of Cork City, which was represented by two MPs, each constituency returned a single member to Westminster. The right to vote was held by householders and by most lodgers, but it was confined to men. This meant that about 15 per cent of the population was entitled to go to the polls. In addition, at this time university representation in parliament was normal; Trinity College, Dublin, returned two members.

This system was overhauled just before the 1918 election. First, Ireland was given two additional seats, which went to the new universities (one each to the National University of Ireland and to Queen's University, Belfast), and minor alterations were made in constituency boundaries. The most significant change, however, was a massive expansion in the electorate. The right to vote was now extended to all men aged at least 21, to women aged 30 or more who were householders or wives of householders, and to soldiers and sailors aged over 18; occupiers of business premises exceeding a certain valuation were allowed one additional vote in certain circumstances. The result was that the electorate increased almost threefold, from less than 700,000 to almost two million; 36 per cent of the new voters were women, 6 per cent military personnel and less than one per cent business voters (see Appendix I).

In fact, the number of first-time voters in Ireland in 1918 was probably even greater than these figures suggest. It was eight years since the previous election in December 1910, but in many constituencies voters had not gone to the polls for a much longer period. In a quarter of the constituencies, the 1918 election was the first to be contested in the twentieth century. In 17 constituencies, the most recent election had taken place in 1892, the year of an exceptionally bitter contest that followed the split over Parnell's leadership and the divorce scandal. The most extreme case was Donegal West, where voters had not gone to the polls in a general election since 1880. Taking these factors into account, and allowing for natural wastage through death, we can estimate that, of the electorate of almost two million, only about 360,000 had previously voted in a parliamentary election.[5]

While these figures do not take account of voting in local elections, they suggest that the electorate of 1918 was for the most part free of previous attachment to any political party. It was therefore in a position to be won over by Sinn Féin. Furthermore, the fact that proportional representation (PR) had not yet been introduced meant that the scale of Sinn Féin's victory would be exaggerated. The actual results illustrate this. In North Leinster, for instance (the counties of Louth, Meath, Westmeath and Longford), Sinn Féin won all five seats under the first-past-the-post system, even though its overall support in this area was only 65 per cent of the vote, to the Nationalists' 35 per cent. If North Leinster had been a five seat constituency under proportional representation, Sinn Féin would probably have won three seats to the Nationalists' two. It is likely that this type of outcome would also have occurred in other parts of the country under PR, resulting in the survival of a sizeable Nationalist Party. As it was, under the existing first-past-the-post system, Sinn Féin was able to win 94 per cent of the contested seats in the 26 counties with only 65 per cent of the vote.

Sinn Féin's pursuit of the nationalist vote was aided by a number of political developments. The first was a tide of public opinion that was rapidly being radicalised. As is generally known, initial public reaction to the 1916 Rising had been largely negative, but this had changed slowly as the British response transformed the executed leaders into martyrs and their imprisoned followers into heroes. Sinn Féin, as we have seen in chapter 2, was able to capitalise on this wave of emotion and to translate it subsequently into a sympathy vote.

A more specific issue also played into Sinn Féin's hands. This was the decision of the British government in April 1918 to make provision for extending conscription to Ireland. On this issue nationalist Ireland was united in its outrage: young Irish men must not be forced to go to war to defend the British Empire. Nationalist politicians of all hues, the Catholic hierarchy and trade union leaders were at one in the vehemence of their objections. So deeply was the issue felt that the Nationalist Party even withdrew from the House of Commons when its protests were disregarded. Despite this radical action by the Nationalists, however, Sinn Féin was able to present itself as the foremost opponent of what a resolution inspired by de Valera described as 'a declaration of war on the Irish nation', 'a violation of the rights of small nationalities' and 'an unwarrantable aggression'.[6]

Even on the land question, which had played so central a role in Nationalist party concerns since the 1880s, the party found itself outflanked by Sinn Féin. While Sinn Féin had always been preoccupied with the political aspects of the Anglo-Irish relationship, the involvement of many of its local activists on the issue of land reform, and the militancy with which this was expressed, helped to undermine the traditional role of the Nationalist party and of the United Irish League.

There was little, indeed, of which the Nationalists could boast in the run-up to the election. They had placed all of their eggs in the Home Rule basket, only to find that there was a hole in the basket. Home Rule, which appeared to have been won in 1914, was postponed. To make matters worse, the partition of Ireland had been placed firmly on the political agenda. The party also suffered, like all parties which have enjoyed a long position of dominance, from allegations of corruption and croneyism. Furthermore, the pattern whereby most constituencies were not contested at general elections had left the party's electoral machinery rather rusty in most parts of the country.[7]

Alongside the tired and demoralised Nationalist Party, Sinn Féin was thus able to project itself as the dynamic force of the future. Not only was it well organised, it could rely on the support of the Irish Volunteers, who, since their military campaign had not yet begun, were free for electioneering. Sinn Féin could also propose a seductively simple solution on the issue of the Anglo-Irish relationship. On winning a majority, it would be in a position to take action on the four points outlined in its election manifesto. These were as follows: first, its representatives would refuse to take their seats in the British parliament; second, the party would use 'any and every means available' to counteract British rule, an implicit statement of acceptance of violent methods; third, Sinn Féin would convene the Irish MPs as a constituent assembly with supreme decision making power; fourth, it would appeal to an international body, the Peace Conference that was shortly to assemble in Paris, for 'the establishment of Ireland as an independent nation'.[8]

The polarisation of public opinion on the issue of self-government for Ireland was so intense that other groups withdrew from the electoral battlefield. In October 1918 the All-for-Ireland League announced its intention not to contest the election (this was the party which, under the leadership of William O'Brien, had broken with the Nationalist Party and had dominated Cork parliamentary representation since 1910). Of potentially wider significance was the position of the Labour Party. Already in September 1918, Labour had decided to contest the post-war election, and its prospects with the huge new electorate appeared good. But it encountered lack of enthusiasm among its own workers, many of whom were sympathetic to Sinn Féin; it was also put under pressure by the Sinn Féin leadership; and Labour itself was divided on matters both of policy and of strategy. Accordingly, in return for some paltry concessions from Sinn Féin, on 1 November it announced its withdrawal from the election and allowed Sinn Féin a clear run, with possible serious long-term consequences for the Labour party itself.

In fact, the only party that was given a slight headache by the Labour movement was the Unionist party in Belfast, where five candidates linked to the British Labour Party went forward. The Unionists easily saw off this challenge, partly by allowing three seats to be taken by candidates proposed by the Ulster Unionist Labour Association, an organisation founded under Carson's prompting to secure working class votes for unionism. Indeed, the Unionists performed exceptionally well in the election, increasing their representation in territorial constituencies to 23 seats.

According to its critics, Sinn Féin was also greatly assisted by its willingness to use unfair or even illegal electioneering tactics. There were many allegations of intimidation of candidates opposed to Sinn Féin and of their workers, and, indeed, of undue pressure on the voters themselves. Allegations of impersonation were similarly widespread. Certain Sinn Féin activists not only admitted to this but even boasted of its extent. As one Sinn Féin supporter in Meath put it: 'I must have voted thirty times at polling booths in our area. But I was not by any means the only one to do so and even the officials were in on it. From midday onwards I used to be greeted with a friendly smile by the presiding officer at a particular booth, and his poll clerk would laughingly ask: "Whose name is it this time?"'[9]

It must nevertheless be pointed out that these practices were commonly to be found at elections not just in Ireland but also elsewhere, and in Ireland they were by no means confined to Sinn Féin.

Whatever about unfair tactics by Sinn Féin, it is clear that the Sinn Féin campaign was itself seriously impeded by government harassment. The election itself was, of course, run by the British government, which was responsible for appointing the officials who administered it (people who themselves were typically Nationalist or Unionist party supporters). In May 1918 the government arrested many of the party's leaders, claiming to have uncovered a 'German plot' involving Sinn Féin. In addition, more than 1,300 republican activists were in prison by the time the election campaign began, its director of elections was arrested, most candidates were either evading arrest or were already under detention, while only 26 Sinn Féin candidates were free to visit their constituencies. The banning of Sinn Féin meetings, the suppression of its election literature and the censorship of its manifesto were further obstacles.

On the other hand, the government's attentions were not entirely unwelcome to the party. The very fact that the British were prepared to go to such lengths to curb Sinn Féin was evidence that the party was to be taken seriously. Ill-treatment by the British was by no means electorally damaging, and being imprisoned was a positive electoral asset to a candidate (as Eoin MacNeill had pointed out to Bulmer Hobson, on the sidelines of the Easter rising, 'We would have no political future if we were not arrested').[10]

The Sinn Féin victory was even more striking given the almost unanimous hostility of the major newspapers. The Irish Times, the (Dublin) Daily Express, the Dublin Evening Mail, the Belfast Newsletter and the Northern Whig supported the Unionist Party, and, of course, dismissed the Sinn Féin programme as being in the world of fantasy. They nevertheless correctly, and rather gleefully, predicted the virtual extinction of the Nationalist Party, and saw the coming electoral contest in stark terms. As the Dublin Daily Express put it in an eve-of-poll editorial, 'The struggle is between anarchy and order, between Bolshevism and progress, between Sinn Féin and Unionism'.[11]

Most of the non-unionist newspapers were committed to supporting the Nationalist Party, and engaged in sharp attacks on Sinn Féin. Editorials, published just before polling began, convey the flavour. According to the Evening Telegraph, Sinn Féin's abstentionist policy was 'the last plank in its almost derelict platform'. The Irish News described the party's policy as making for 'political impotence and national disaster'. The Cork Examiner described Sinn Féin as 'rainbow chasing' after 'a mirage republic'; and the Freeman's Journal, which had a long association with the Nationalist Party, dismissed Sinn Féin promises, praising instead the constitutional nationalist tradition. Only the Irish Independent and the Evening Herald softened the anti-Sinn Féin tone, the latter advising its readers to assess candidates on their merits, culminating in a slogan that was not exceptionally helpful, 'Vote for Ireland'.[12]

Except in the case of the university constituencies, where polling lasted for five days and the count began immediately on close of polling, there was a long postponement of the count. This was occasioned by the need to wait for delivery of the votes of soldiers who were still on the western front, and resulted in a two-week delay. In the event, the soldiers' votes, while they would be unlikely to help Sinn Féin, are unlikely to have damaged that party either, due to the low turnout of this group. Two random examples illustrate the position: in Cork City only 27 per cent of the absent soldiers and sailors voted, while in Roscommon South the figure was 32 per cent.[13]

The response of the press to the election results reflected the political divisions of Irish society. The unionist press interpreted the results as putting a nail in the coffin of the Nationalist Party and, rather perversely, took the view that the Union was thereby strengthened. The nationalist newspapers, in chastened editorials, pointed to the heavy responsibility that now lay on the shoulders of the newly elected deputies but accepted the results as a legitimate and decisive victory for Sinn Féin. As the Freeman's Journal put it:

'The meaning of the Irish vote is as clear as it is emphatic. More than two thirds of the electors throughout Nationalist Ireland have endorsed the Sinn Féin programme. Whatever may be said of the methods employed by them in most constituencies to secure a majority it cannot be denied that they put before the electors a straight issue. They invited the people to vote the demand for an independent Irish Republic, completely separated from Great Britain ... Whatever democratic Nationalists may think of the wisdom of the people's decision, whatever their doubts about the practicability of the Republican policy, ... as democrats, Nationalists are bound now to give the Republicans a fair field.'[14]

The intensity of the contest in Ireland between Sinn Féin and the Nationalists has attracted so much attention that it is easy to overlook the broader context of the 1918 election. The election had been called, after all, to return a new British parliament, not to permit the convening of the first Dáil. In Great Britain voters had, indeed, shown a considerable degree of volatility, but it was established parties rather than new parties that had profited. The main immediate beneficiary of the franchise extension in Britain was, in fact, the Conservative party. It won a clear parliamentary majority (though on a share of the vote that had fallen to 39.6 per cent, from 46.6 percent in 1910); the seats won by the 'Lloyd George Liberals', a faction of the Liberal Party that was in coalition with the Conservatives, brought an extra 12.6 per cent of the votes and ensured the coalition an overwhelming parliamentary majority, placing it in a strong position for its coming battle with Irish nationalism in the form of Sinn Féin and the first Dáil. The Liberal Party proper had dropped from 44.2 to 13.0 per cent, while Labour had risen from 6.4 to 21.4 per cent, but the two parties were unable to muster even 100 MPs between them.

The 1918 election also needs to be seen in a broader European context. The sharp increase in support for radical parties and policies immediately after the First World War was not confined to Ireland. The dislocation of war, the collapse of the old social order and the climate of political change had brought radical groups to the forefront in other countries too. This was especially true of the powers defeated in the war, and of the newly-emerging independent states of central and eastern Europe. Although Ireland's war-time experience had been significantly different, the outcome was similar: a popular appetite for revolutionary change. As the conservative press warned, the 'virus' of bolshevism was at large, and not even Ireland was spared.

How are the results of the 1918 election in Ireland to be interpreted? Was it, as one set of critics pointed out, a confidence trick by Sinn Féin, which was leading the unsuspecting public along what it claimed was the road to the republic, but which was in fact luring them down a political cul-de-sac? Or was it, as Sinn Féin activists claimed, a massive popular endorsement of the policy of the republic?

The verdict of historians and, indeed, of most contemporary observers was that, whatever blemishes marred the election campaign, the people had been offered a clear-cut choice. Their decision had been equally clear-cut. The strongly partisan nature of the contest is best illustrated by the result in Cork City, where each of the 31,000 people who voted was entitled to vote for two candidates. There were six candidates whose names appeared on the ballot paper in alphabetical order, without indication of party (in fact, there were two candidates from each of the three major parties). In the event, 94 per cent of voters filled in their ballot papers along strict party lines, opting for two candidates of the same party; only 4 per cent voted for candidates of two different parties, while 2 per cent were 'plumpers' who voted for one candidate only.15 Given the contemporary emphasis on the plebiscitary character of the election, this represented a significant victory for Sinn Féin's policy of self-determination, though the election also confirmed the existence in Ulster of areas of entrenched opposition to any form of Irish self-government.

This is not to say that the new Irish voters of 1918 had carefully weighed the consequences of their votes; like electors everywhere, emotion and instinct played a great part in their decision. Research into voting behaviour suggests that, even in western democracies where the overall level of education is higher than in the Ireland of 1918, voters' views tend to be unstructured and inconsistent over time:

'This view, that the great majority of voters were simply too ignorant of the issues of the day and too ill-equipped conceptually to deal with complex political issues, came to be widely accepted as an accurate picture of the British, as of the American, voter in the 1960s. The 'ideal' voter of liberal democratic theory – concerned, informed, basing party choice upon a careful weighing-up of the parties' positions on important issues of the day – was consigned to the political theory textbook.'[16]

It is not to be expected that the new Irish electorate of 1918, however well informed politically many of its members might have been, was fundamentally more sophisticated than the contemporary electorate. While this does not undermine the overwhelming nature of the Sinn Féin mandate, this more sceptical interpretation was articulated at the time by a prominent Sinn Féin member, Father O'Flanagan: 'The people have voted Sinn Féin. What we have to do now is to explain to them what Sinn Féin is'.17 This task, together with others more daunting, would fall on the shoulders of the newly elected Sinn Féin MPs. This key group of people forms the subject of the next chapter.

Notes

Acknowledgement. I would like to acknowledge the assistance of Professor T P O'Neill in commenting on an earlier draft.

1. P S O'Hegarty, The Victory of Sinn Féin: How it Won it, and How it Used it (Dublin: Talbot Press, 1924), p. 30.
2. The definitive statement of this argument will be found in Seymour Martin Lipset and Stein Rokkan, 'Cleavage structures, party systems and voter alignments: an introduction', pp. 1-64 in Seymour M Lipset and Stein Rokkan (eds) Party Systems and Voter Alignments: Cross-National Perspectives (New York: The Free Press, 1967). Lipset and Rokkan argued essentially that European party systems had tended to 'fossilise' at around the period when substantial mass suffrage was introduced (typically, this was shortly after the First World War).
3. Of the 103 Irish seats, the Nationalists held 85 in 1885, 84 in 1886, 81 (including five independent nationalists) in 1900, 82 (including one independent nationalist) in 1906, 81 (including 11 supporters of William O'Brien's All-for-Ireland League) in January 1910 and 83 (including 10 O'Brienites) in December 1910. In 1892 the party had been divided between 71 anti-Parnellites and nine Parnellites; in 1895 between 69 anti-Parnellites and 12 Parnellites.
4. Of the 77 Nationalists in the outgoing parliament, nine were independent nationalist followers of William O'Brien. The outgoing Irish representation also included 18 Unionists and two Liberals.
5. Calculated from Brian M Walker (ed.), Parliamentary Election Results in Ireland, 1801-1922 (Dublin: Royal Irish Academy, 1978), by computing the number of persons who voted at the previous contested parliamentary election in each constituency and estimating the number of survivors on the basis of a very crude measure, an annual mortality rate of 2%.
6. Dorothy Macardle, The Irish Republic (London: Corgi, 1968; first ed. 1937), p. 233.

7. Of 101 Irish constituencies, the numbers for which MPs were returned unopposed at general elections were as follows: 1885, 21; 1886, 68; 1892, 20; 1895, 60; 1900, 70; 1906, 80; January 1910, 64; December 1910, 63.
8. The text of the manifesto is reproduced in Macardle, Irish Republic, pp 842-4.
9. Cited in R. F. Foster, Modern Ireland 1600-1972 (London: Penguin, 1989; first ed., 1988), p. 638.
10. Foster, Modern Ireland, p. 491.
11. Daily Express, 13 December 1918.
12. All on 13 or 14 December 1918.
13. Cork Examiner, 30 December 1918; Roscommon Messenger, 4 January 1919.
14. 30 December 1918.
15. Calculated from Cork Examiner, 30 December 1918.
16. David Denver and Gordon Hands (eds), Issues and Controversies in British Electoral Behaviour (London: Harvester Wheatsheaf, 1992), p. 171. The subsequent debate on this issue has not been conclusive in undermining this view.
17. O'Hegarty, Victory of Sinn Féin, p. 32.

4

The Formation of the Irish Political Élite

Tom Garvin

Dr Tom Garvin is Professor of Politics in University College, Dublin. He is the author of many studies in Irish politics and comparative politics. He is the author of *The Evolution of Irish Nationalist Politics*, Dublin 1981, and *Nationalist Revolutionaries in Ireland*, Oxford 1988. He is at present working on a study of the emergence of modern Irish democracy.

◆◆◆◆◆◆◆◆◆◆

The Republic of Ireland is unusual among the older English-speaking western democracies in being not only democratic, but in being born of violent revolution. Democratic politicians like Kevin O'Higgins went, with an extraordinary symmetry, with apparently romantic revolutionaries like Michael Collins. Only the United States among this small group of post-England countries has a similar post-revolutionary heritage. Further, the Irish revolution was heavily informed by its American predecessor, a fact that has been overlooked, almost to the level of intellectual incompetence or irresponsibility, by some historians of Ireland.

The Fenians of the 1860s, for example, used songs derived from the songs of the soldiers of the American Civil War; Fenian leaders were often prominent American Civil War veterans, and were 'the men in the square-toed boots,' or men who wore Yankee Army shoes. Again, Charles Stewart Parnell, a man with an anglophobic American mother, counted heavily on American-Irish goodwill and dollars. American money also fuelled the Irish War of Independence; Kevin O'Shiel, one of the first Dáil judges, wrote a history of the American revolution in the middle of the Irish revolution. He was very clearly fascinated by the analogy between the Yankee Minutemen and the IRA of his own time.[1]

The fact that violence played an important part in the formation of the Irish democracy between 1913 and 1923 has had serious consequences for Irish political culture. For example, the romantic rhetoric of militarist nationalism had to be paid homage to by civilian, elected politicians long after the militaristic phase of the revolution was over. Even now, three-quarters of a century on, the way in which the Rising of 1916 should be commemorated is not quite a dead issue.

The fact that nationalist violence during that period was a rather reluctant reaction to the Ulster rebellion against Home Rule in 1912 has also been significant; the relationships between the two states that emerged in Ireland after 1920 were, for a long time, centred in an historically shared set of wishes that London favour one Irish step-daughter of Empire over the other. In the first generation after independence, the North was clearly favoured both psychologically and financially. Even nowadays, this competition between North and South for London's favour goes on to some extent; clearly, a stereotypically 'genial' South is now winning over an equally stereotypical 'grim' North that was for so long favoured.

The most obvious consequence of the violence incurred during the birth of the Irish Free State was the split between those who supported the use of non-violent, constitutional means of political action and those who saw violence as the principle way in which nationalist aspirations could be achieved. Eamon de Valera was to spend much of his career in trying to bridge that division; either in trying to legitimise the revolution or in trying to avoid it.[2]

The leaders who created the revolution and who both led the armed struggle and created a democratic order shared this deep ambivalence about politics and violence. They were often simultaneously national democrats and national insurrectionists, and the division was commonly inside each leader's mind. Michael Collins, for example, was a man of often ruthless violence who made an astonishing transition to something like statesmanship in 1921-22; Eamon de Valera, the hero of 1916, was to make a slower, but fundamentally similar, transition between 1919 and 1936. The general pattern of younger gunman evolving into older politician is very striking.

The tradition which the revolutionary élite came from was that of the Irish Republican Brotherhood. The IRB, or Fenian Brotherhood, dated back to 1858, and was founded by three men who met in Langan's Timber Yard in what is now Fenian Street in Dublin. The word 'Fenian' itself recalled hazy notions of the Fianna of Fionn Mac Cumhaill. The Fenians had enjoyed extensive support among Irish emigrants in the United States in particular. Many of its founders had emigrated to the United States, commonly in the shadow of the Great Famine. Many of these early Fenians were imbued with a vision of Ireland as a country that England, as an empire, had ruined. An abortive rising was staged by some Fenians in 1867. Later, Fenian activists were heavily involved in agrarian politics and nationalist movements of all sorts. One could claim that old Fenians constructed much of the modern Irish party system.

By the end of the nineteenth century, however, the Fenian movement appeared to be moribund, and was seemingly dominated by old men who reportedly bored their younger fellow countrymen with reminiscences of their rebel youth. Young men were more interested in joining the British Army, getting an education or simply emigrating to America. However, political events in the period after the fall of Parnell revived the old movement's flagging fortunes.

First of all, Parnell's destruction appeared to discredit, and certainly weakened, constitutional nationalism of the kind that he had offered the nationalist Irish. Secondly, the rise of two key organisations, one sporting and one cultural, gave the IRB leaders their chance. The sporting organisation was, of course, the Gaelic

Athletic Association, founded in Thurles in 1884 and dedicated to the revival and development of Gaelic games. The IRB quickly penetrated the organisation and used it as a propaganda vehicle and as a way of getting into the minds of young people. In particular, the GAA was used to drive a wedge between the young men and the police, as well as segregating the young men from British armed forces personnel. Members of these forces were excluded by the GAA from its activities, and the GAA also prohibited its members from participating in what were called 'foreign games:' games such as rugby and soccer.[3]

This division between young men who 'took the King's shilling' and those who refused to take it, sometimes because they could afford not to, became very deep, and often served as a alibi for murdering ex-servicemen in 1919-23.[4] This same division tended, despite the IRB's essential ideological liberalism, to coincide with the older Catholic versus Protestant divisions on the island. Radical Catholics became attracted to republicanism or socialism; radical Protestants became attracted to liberal unionism or 'British' socialism.

The cultural organisation was the Gaelic League, founded in Dublin in 1893. The League was dedicated to the rediscovery of Gaelic Ireland, and to the revival of as much of Ireland's traditional culture as was feasible. Also, it wished to clean up aspects of Gaelic culture that were unacceptable to late Victorian morals. The version of Gaelic culture that it offered had at best a very curious relationship to the real, semi-pagan, Gaelic culture that it claimed to be defending. The Gaelic League became very popular after 1900, having been mainly a Dublin and Trinity College coterie up to then. Eventually this organisation was to come under the control of the IRB in 1911, a power-grab being engineered by Thomas Ashe and Sean T O'Kelly. This was much to the distress of the League's founder, Douglas Hyde, who profoundly disliked his organisation being penetrated by politics.[5]

Another event which gave new heart to the younger nationalist revolutionaries was the Boer War. The spectacle of two small Boer republics fighting the British Empire to a standstill seemed to indicate that the age of imperialism was coming to an end. Britain was a superpower, but was not without rivals. Germany constituted a major, and growing menace on the European mainland, and the United States was already showing signs of developing the military and industrial might which later permitted it to slip into Britain's seat as the new hegemonic world power in the twentieth century.

The IRB, the Gaelic League, the Dungannon Clubs and the Gaelic Athletic Association attracted large numbers of young men and women in the first years of the new century, much as was happening to similar organisations elsewhere in Europe. The decade before 1914 was a time of a youth cult throughout Europe. In Germany, romantic nature-loving organisations such as the Wandervoegel proliferated. In England, young people joined extra-mural educational schemes, recorded lovingly in the writings of, for example, H G Wells. In Ireland, the IRB and similar organisations, both unionist and nationalist, recruited many energetic young men, disillusioned with politics and possessed of a cult of heroism and violence. Young women followed enthusiastically after, often urging the young men on.

Meanwhile, constitutionalism had become shipwrecked yet again in Ireland. In 1912, Ulster prepared openly to resist Home Rule by force if need be, with support from elements in the British Army. Ulster Unionism also had the help of many senior Tories. A major historical irony is provided by the fact that Ulster 'loyalists' were also aided by the Imperial German Government, fishing in the troubled waters of a potential enemy. Ulster loyalism originated in the deepest of treasons. Many heroic supporters of Ulster loyalism and unionism were massacred during the First World War, most spectacularly at the Battle of the Somme, in mid-1916.

In 1913, the Irish Volunteers, heavily penetrated by the IRB, arose to counter the Ulster Volunteers. The Irish Volunteers were explicitly inspired by their Ulster counterparts. The coming of the Great War left the secret society in control of about five thousand separatist and anti-War Volunteers. This military organisation was the immediate ancestor of the Irish Republican Army and, strangely, of the Army of the independent Irish state that emerged in 1922.

The IRB, a small group of men, now had its own little army, but inside this conspiratorial group lay a further conspiracy, centred on Patrick Pearse. This even smaller group staged a rebellion in Dublin in 1916, against the wishes of the majority of the IRB leadership. After the executions and the attempt by London to impose conscription in 1918, separatism in the form of Sinn Féin swept nationalist Ireland. The new party won virtually all seats in Ireland outside eastern Ulster in the British general election of December 1918. The new MPs refused to take their seats in Westminster, and declared themselves to be the democratically elected rulers of a putatively independent Ireland.

Dáil Éireann was founded in January 1919. Guerrilla war followed, and in 1922 Britain conceded effective independence to twenty-six of Ireland's thirty-two counties. This compromise split the independence movement totally, and a short civil war in the South resulted in the defeat of the insurrectionists by the compromisers.

In the remainder of this talk, I will present a social analysis of the IRB, Sinn Féin and IRA élite as it was on the eve of coming to state power in 1922. I define the élite as including all Sinn Féin and Republican Labour TDs elected in 1918 or 1921, in republican reckoning the First and Second Dáils; all IRA leaders listed in the standard *Who's Who of the War of Independence*; all Cumann na mBan leaders similarly included; all members of the Supreme Council of the IRB, 1920, and all sixteen leaders executed in 1916. The élite thus defined comes to 304 people.[6]

One salient feature of the nationalist leadership was, unsurprisingly, youth. Most were born in the 1880s and 1890s, with a noticeable bias in favour of the later decade. Most were male, and they were nearly all Catholic. Proportionately speaking, the group was far more Catholic than was the population of the island of Ireland at that time, as nearly one quarter of the population was Protestant, mainly, but not entirely, concentrated in Ulster. The élite was very clearly non-northern; the six counties which came to make up Northern Ireland were dramatically under-represented, and this was so even if only the Catholic population of the area were to be taken into account.

A very large proportion of the leaders had some experience in the Gaelic League, which provided them with an ideology of loyalty to the past, to cultural roots and to the idea of reviving the ancestral Irish culture. Most paid at least lip-service to the project of making the Irish language once again the main spoken language of the island. Many went farther than that, and became very proficient speakers of the language and enthusiastic, even fanatical, proponents of its revival.

The Gaelic League appears to have had a huge 'spiritual' or psychological impact on that generation of young men and women. It was, in a sense, their university and their movement of personal liberation. In old age, veterans of the movement would reminisce wistfully about the expeditions to archaeological sites, the ceilidhes, the language classes and the national conventions that brought thousands of young men and women together in Dublin every year. In a country which was rather dull, conformist and repressive, the League appeared to supply a way of sharing patriotic projects, an intellectual life and a cultural rediscovery. It was also a means of getting away from parental control, and the restrictions which priests and employers attempted to impose on young people.

Even if we leave the six counties of what is now Northern Ireland out of account completely, the leadership was pronouncedly southern in origin. It was southern even in relation to the twenty-six county area that became the Irish Free State. The southern province of Munster was noticeably favoured as the place of origin of the revolutionary leaders. The Dublin area was the birthplace, or place of early rearing, of only one-sixth of the leaders; the rest of Leinster had a proportionate number of birthplaces, but Munster, with well over one third of the leaders, was very heavily over-represented. Cork was, even in Munster, heavily over represented, and west Cork was particularly prominent as a producer of leaders: Michael Collins, Gearoid O'Sullivan, J J Walsh, Diarmuid O'Hegarty and Tom Barry were among the most conspicuous members of this very conspicuous group.

As in many other nationalist movements, leaders tended to come from either rural areas or very large towns. Relatively few came from the small towns that dominated so much of the country commercially and militarily, serving as they did as bases for military garrisons and the barracks of the Royal Irish Constabulary. Sinn Féin's top leaders, often first generation city folk, joined hands with rural activists against the towns. Ernie O'Malley, author of what is perhaps the most literary IRA reminiscence of that time *On Another Man's Wound*, wrote 'In the country the small farmers and labourers were our main support, and in cities the workers with a middle-class sprinkling; towns we could not rely on.'

This pattern was repeated in the financing of the movement. Contributions to the cause of Irish independence were noticeably more generous in the province of Munster, Limerick being particularly open-handed. This southern bias was not new. It appears to echo the distribution of the Gaelic League, in many ways the key founding organisation, which was very strong in Munster. Munster had been the home of the early GAA, and had a tradition of rural agitation and violence which dated back to the middle of the eighteenth century. Whiteboyism, an extraordinary series of agrarian organisations, for example, started in Tipperary, in central Munster, in 1760, in the middle of the Seven Years War. Munster was also the province of origin of the Christian Brothers, an educational order which had an immeasurable effect on the minds of thousands of young, able and ambitious men in the last decades of British rule.

Rurality was a noticeable feature of Irish political organisations in general. Many Sinn Féin or IRA leaders tended to have local power bases in country areas where they had many relatives and were regarded as part of the local community. If they left their native areas, it was not to go to neighbouring counties where they might be resented as blow-ins, but rather to go to Dublin or farther afield. De Valera goes from Bruree to Dublin, Collins goes from Sam's Cross to London. Country-born men in Dublin had the advantage relative to native-born Dubliners of being 'county men', with access to an informal freemasonry based on links of kinship, schooling and place.

In many ways, Munster was the part of Ireland which had become closest to true independence prior to 1914. The novels of Charles Kickham and Canon Sheehan, which enjoyed an enormous popularity at that time, extolled the virtues of the rural, familial and yeoman-farmer society that had emerged in Munster in particular in the post Famine era. In some ways, this ideological preference for rural and familial society echoed Thomas Jefferson's similar idealisation of the American yeoman farmer a century previously. In some ways, Sinn Féin became dominated by Munster elements. It was in Munster that the bulk of the IRA campaign against British authority became most intense, it was the fighting men of Munster who resisted most stubbornly the Treaty settlement, and it was in western Munster that the anti-Treatyites made their last stand in 1923. On the other hand, the 'west Cork Mafia' centred on Michael Collins was a crucial support for the infant Free State at the beginning.

Occupationally, the leaders of the independence movement were middle-class, as is usual among revolutionary leaders everywhere. Furthermore, those who were of humbler origin were evidently clever, energetic and very upwardly mobile. The professions were heavily represented, both the higher professions such as medicine or law, and the lower professions such as teaching and journalism; these were people who dealt in ideas and in publicising such ideas. Civil servants and shopkeepers were noticeably well represented. Farmers were not as well-represented as might be expected from their presence in the general population. Over half the population of the twenty-six counties were engaged in farming at that time, but only one fifth of the leaders seem to have been farmers. However, a very large proportion of the leaders had parents who were farmers.

To sum it up, the leaders were non-agrarian and middle class, highly educated by the standards of the time, socially mobile and probably unusually energetic and intellectually able. Nearly half had received some third level education, a statistically extraordinary proportion at that time. Many Sinn Féin and IRA leaders were students at, or recent graduates of, the new university colleges and teacher training institutes that had sprung up to give a first generation of Catholics a third level education of a kind acceptable to their religious beliefs.

Another feature of the leaders was their relative cosmopolitanism. Perhaps half of the leaders had lived outside Ireland for significant portions of their lives, usually in Britain or the United States. The 'returned emigrant' syndrome, so conspicuous in the Fenianism of the 1860s, was very noticeable in the leadership of the movement. Foreign experience does seem to have had a stimulating effect on these young men; Collins was a voracious reader of the kind of English literature an intelligent young man of the time would have read: Wells, Galsworthy, Bennett and Shaw. P S O'Hegarty, another Corkman and one-time employee of the Post Office in London, was secularised by his experiences; unlike many of the leaders, he supported a complete and unambiguous separation of Church and State, and ascribed his opinion to his experience of living in secular London.

In many cases, living in England moderated the young men's inherited anglophobia. It may be, for example, that Collins' extraordinary turnaround on the Treaty issue was partly due to his understanding of, and liking for, the English leaders, an understanding and liking which de Valera apparently did not share. De Valera had never lived in England, whereas Collins had spent nearly ten years in London. De Valera had the advantage of a Blackrock College education but Collins had the clear advantage of an education in the brilliant national school system of the time.

The split of 1922 seems to have been only mildly conditioned by these sociological characteristics of the leaders. In fact, the best predictor of the vote on the Treaty was sex; all six women TDs voted against the Treaty in January 1922, and a lot of incidental evidence indicates that women activists were far more likely to oppose the Treaty than were men. Why this was so is hard to say, but may have had something to do with political selection. In the Victorian culture of the time, it was unusual for women to engage in public political activity. Any woman who did choose to do so would, therefore, be defying a strong taboo, and be perhaps more adventurous or radical than the average male activist. Certainly, the radicalism of the women was noted at the time; the anti-Treatyites became known humorously as 'The Women and Childers Party.' Eskine Childers, a famous half-English activist, got typed, together with the 'republican women' as a prime wrecker of the Treaty. It is intriguing to speculate as to how much of the intense reaction against women in public life after 1922 was generated by the behaviour of the 'republican women' in 1921-23.

Another striking aspect of the split of 1922 was how it had the power to split families. For example, brothers in the MacNeill family fought on opposite sides, as did brothers of the well-known west Cork Hales family, to take two random instances of a common phenomenon. Older leaders supported the Treaty more firmly than did the young.

Overall, the impression given is that the Treaty divided people by personal loyalty to one or other of the top leadership rather than by social origin. Collins' acceptance of the Treaty was the main factor which induced his famous squad to accept it too and form the core of the new Free State Army. A common remark was to the effect that 'if it's good enough for Mick, it's good enough for me.' Similarly, de Valera's abrupt rejection of the Treaty turned many key figures against it. Harry Boland actually admitted he opposed the Treaty because he could not let de Valera down in his time of crisis. A certain feminist solidarity with her fellow woman TDs seems to have persuaded Dr Ada English to oppose the Treaty. De Valera's personal trust in the advice of Erskine Childers, together with his evident fondness for the Englishman, seem to have been significant factors in prompting him to reject the settlement.

Personal loyalties have as much to do with collective political action as do ideological systems of belief or class solidarities. The split of 1922 was partly ideological, but seems to have been an intensely personal division between people who had been comrades together in a collective revolutionary experience which was extraordinarily intense. The split was experienced not just as a parting of the ways, but as a moral collapse, the destruction of a great solidarity which would never be rebuilt.

The other side of the coin in such a sub-culture was, of course, disloyalty, whether actual or perceived. Each side increasingly accused the other not of being misguided, but of disloyalty, whether that be disloyalty to the Republic or to a Treaty that was held to be in Ireland's national interest. Dialogue between the two sides became impossible, as mutual distrust took over from the extraordinary comradeship of the previous six years. Irish democracy had a bloody birth in 1922, as the new Army of the Irish Free State under Collins and Richard Mulcahy crushed an IRA that was seen as being in mutiny against a democratically elected Dáil Éireann.

Subsequently, the two sides formed stable political parties which have dominated the politics of independent Ireland ever since. The bitterness caused by the Civil War took fifty years to fade. However, behind the hatreds there does seem to have been a certain sense of collective shame, as though the Irish Civil War had been unnecessary, a disaster that had befallen both sides.

Furthermore, almost like quarrelsome children, they had broken the toy which they had all coveted and over which they had quarrelled: the vision of an independent, thirty-two county Ireland. Whatever chance there was of the Treaty settlement achieving some all-Ireland arrangement disappeared in the violence of a Civil War that was mainly fought in Munster, a province that was physically and mentally remote from Ulster.

The gradual realisation of the elementary proposition of the futility of the Civil War sobered the new Irish national political élite mightily, and helped to turn visionaries into sadder, bitterer but perhaps wiser men and women. These new élites set themselves to build a consensual democracy, with all its faults and limitations, on the part of the island of Ireland they had inherited. However, because of this embittered past, Dublin politicians proved incapable of handling the Northern Ireland problem, until that first generation of élites had died out and politicians who did not know about, or care about, the ephemeral issues of 1922 eventually took over.

Notes

1. Kevin O'Sheil, *The Birth of a Republic*, Dublin: Talbot Press, 1920; The standard book on the emergence of the Free State is Joseph Curran, *The Birth of the Irish Free State*, Alabama: Alabama University Press, 1980, which has never been published in Ireland. This tells one much about Irish publishers. See my *Nationalist Revolutionaries in Ireland*, Oxford: Oxford University Press, 1987. Also see the essays in Theo Dorgan and Máirín ní Dhonaghadha, *Revising the Rising*, Derry: Field Day, 1991.

2. Sean Cronin, *The McGarrity Papers*, Tralee: Anvil, 1972, 151-74.

3. Tom Garvin, *The Evolution of Irish Nationalist Politics*, Dublin,: Gill and Macmillan, 1981, 135-59.

4. On ex-servicemen as targets, Peter Hart, *The IRA and its Enemies*, draft book in private possession, *passim*.

5. Tom Garvin, 'The Politics of Languages and Literature,' Irish Political Studies, Vol 2 (1987), 49 64; Diarmuid Lynch, *The IRB and the 1916 Insurrection*, Cork: Mercier, 1957, *passim*.

6. Elite sources: Flynn's *Parliamentary Companion*, Dublin: Stationery Office, 1929, 1932, 1939, 1945; H Boylan, *Dictionary of National Biography*; P O'Farrell, *Who's Who in the Irish War of Independence*, Dublin and Cork: Mercier, 1980. On élite analysis, Tom Garvin, *Nationalist Revolutionaries in Ireland*, Oxford: Oxford University Press, 1987, 33-55; see also, Al Cohan, *The Irish Political Elite*, Dublin: Gill and Macmillan, 1972.

5

The First Dáil and its
Constitutional Documents

Brian Farrell

The best-known and most frequently quoted document produced by the First Dáil was the 'Democratic Programme'.[1] This was a radically egalitarian, socially advanced, economically focused statement of objectives. It consciously echoed the words of Pearse in the Easter Proclamation of 1916 and re-affirmed Connolly's mix of nationalism and socialism. Its very first sentence declared:

The right of the people of Ireland to the ownership of Ireland........ that the Nation's sovereignty extends not only to all men and women of the Nation, but to all its material possessions, the Nation's soil and all its resources, all the wealth and wealth-producing processes within the Nation and with [Pearse] we reaffirm that all right to private property must be subordinated to the public right and welfare.

This was the rhetoric of progressive social democracy. The 'Democratic Programme' was promising not only a new political order but a new type of society. There was the promise that 'no child shall suffer hunger or cold from lack of food, clothing or shelter.' The existing Poor Law System was to be replaced by an extensive welfare and health scheme. Implicitly these reforms, sketched in the First Dáil's 'Democratic Programme', were to be financed by extensive governmental intervention in economic development.

It shall be our duty to promote the development of the Nation's resources, to increase the productivity of its soil, to exploit its mineral deposits, peat bogs and fisheries, its waterways and harbours, in the interests of and for the benefit of the Irish people.

All of this promised an intellectual analysis, economic practice and social reconstruction that would have revolutionised early twentieth-century Ireland. It would have transformed the independence project into a social revolution. But that did not happen. For the 'Democratic Programme' had never represented the real aspirations of the First Dáil created by Sinn Féin. It was only one of four constitutional documents adopted unanimously and without debate at the very first day's meeting. A closer examination of all four, and the circumstances of their drafting, provides a more accurate interpretation of a far less radically inclined party and parliamentary assembly.

The very speed with which Sinn Féin grew into a broad-based national organisation had left little time to consider policy development. On the thorniest question of all – whether it was to be committed, in the old IRB formula, to a republic virtually established – de Valera's masterly compromise postponed division. The formula read:

Sinn Féin aims at securing the international recognition of Ireland as an independent Irish Republic. Having achieved that status the Irish people may by Referendum freely choose their form of government.

It knitted together the ideals of committed republicans like Brugha and the constitutionalists who followed Griffith's more sophisticated model. It was enough to satisfy, for the moment, the diverse strands that made up the new Sinn Féin. If they were prepared to postpone consideration of the central political issue confronting the emerging new Ireland, they had little time or inclination to examine questions of economic and social policy that would inevitably expose other divisions in their ranks.

The central purpose was to assist a unified claim to independence. In the crowded years between the conscription crisis and the creation of the First Dáil the leaders of Sinn Féin kept their sights firmly fixed on that objective. The minute books of the National Executive are full of detailed discussions regarding electoral arrangements, party organisation, candidate selection. Occasionally there are questions about North-East Ulster and attempts to devise a strategy. But there is no discussion of shaping a vision of the kind of Irish society that might emerge after independence.

The Labour Party, for its part, was fully alert to the possibilities created by the introduction of a popular franchise.[2] It recognised, in O'Casey's phrase, 'Labour will have to fight Sinn Féin'. Labour activists were more keenly aware than Sinn Féin's new recruits that Griffith was no friend of theirs. One Labour pamphleteer wrote that Sinn Féin is:

... complex, subtle and contradictory. It is but the new name for developed capitalism in Ireland, using nationality and the Irish language as a cloak to reach its goal... what the Irish Republic the Sinn Féiners are after is but the counterpart of France and America where year after year the capitalist sweats dividends out of his helpless workers.

So, throughout 1918, Labour prepared to contest the forthcoming general election as an independent political party. Manifestos were prepared, candidates chosen in carefully selected and winnable constituencies.

At a two-day meeting of the National Executive in September an agreed resolution spelled out:

Our object in entering upon the contest is to provide an opportunity for the workers to prove their adhesion to the principles and policy of the Labour Party, to strengthen the position of Irish Labour in its relations with the international Labour movement, and to prepare the way for a full representation of Labour in any future Irish Parliament.

But obstacles soon blocked the way to Labour's parliamentary representation in Ireland. The question of abstention from Westminster threatened to split Northern Labour. Negotiations to agree an electoral pact with Sinn Féin in Dublin bred accusations and suspicions. In many parts of the country trade unionists were persuaded that Labour should not disrupt a unified push to achieve independence. There was also at least some intimidation to encourage Labour supporters to stay in line with Sinn Féin.

Eventually, at a Special Conference in November 1918, the question of Labour contesting the general election was resolved. Faced with a variety of internal divisions – geographic, ideological, cultural and generational – the National Executive reversed its earlier position and recommended that Labour withdraw. Party leader Thomas Johnson offered a subtle, but scarcely convincing, rationale for this about-turn. Much had happened in the previous six weeks, he argued. Labour had originally intended to contest a war-time election; now it would be a peace election. He went on:

A call comes from all parts of Ireland for a demonstration of unity on this question of self-determination, such as was witnessed on the conscription issue. Your executive believes that the workers of Ireland join earnestly in this desire, that they would willingly sacrifice, for a brief period, their aspirations towards political power.

Johnson said enough to sway the majority. Labour withdrew from the election. But the new Dáil owed it some recompense and the bill would soon be presented.

Meantime, Sinn Féin was deprived of many of its most prominent and experienced leaders as they were rounded up following discovery of the so-called 'German Plot'. This might have provoked a mood of intransigent extremism among those left behind. That shrewd observer Tim Healy wrote to his parliamentary party friend William O'Brien:

The Shin [sic] chiefs being quodded it is only natural that the subs should be as unbending as a C.C. might be if the Pope and Curia were under duress. One of them told me things would come right but they are so headless, folly is sure to come uppermost.[3]

O'Brien was less pessimistic after a meeting with Fr O'Flanagan but responded later:

I understand and share all your anxieties as to the chaos at S.F. headquarters and the possibility of insane councils getting the upperhand..... the mad men are undoubtedly there and English treachery is giving them every possible justification.

But these old-style parliamentarians were far removed from the new élite that was busily elbowing them off the political stage. There were outsiders, dependent on newspapers and gossip. They found it difficult to accept or understand that the new generation of leaders who were displacing them were, in fact, potentially politicians much like themselves.

The Sinn Féin representatives still at large who were free to organise and sit at the first meeting of the First Dáil were far removed from the stereotype of revolutionary extremist or guerilla freedom fighter. Taken together with the Sinn Féin Executive of the time they were a group of men and women certainly committed to securing immediate independence but moderate and realistic in their perceptions of what that independence might mean. Their moderation is reflected in the basic constitutional documents that they drafted and adopted.

The initiative in arranging the Dáil's inauguration was taken at the Sinn Féin National Executive's weekly meeting on 19 December 1918. The wording of the minutes show how readily Sinn Féin slipped into parliamentary usage, how willingly the conventions of parliamentary government were accepted. Beasley and Collins were 'deputed to issue the whip to the Republican members.... it was decided to refer to the [sic] Dáil Éireann the question of its machinery and functions, and the future relations between it and the Standing Committee.' Somewhat optimistically it was planned that there would be a joint meeting of the party executive and Dáil members on New Year's Day and the Dáil would meet publicly on the following day. In the event, it took a little longer.

The joint meeting on 1 January 1919 referred three items to a secret meeting of Dáil representatives a week later. These items were: to determine the relationship between the party and parliament; the issue of a Declaration of Independence; and, the issue of a Message to the Free Nations of the World (that is, to the

League of Nations). The further secret meeting on 7 January was a parliament in miniature, following established Westminster procedures through a carefully organised 'Order of the Day'. These included formal motions to appoint 'select committees' to draw up a constitution, the Declaration of Independence and the Message to the Free Nations. There was, as yet, no mention of any 'Democratic Programme'. But at a further meeting a week later it was announced that a document drafted by the Irish Workers' delegation of the International [Socialist] Conference was submitted to the members present, and it was decided that the statement of national claims set out was heartily approved. A committee was appointed to:

... draw up the draft of a programme of constructive work on democratic lines in consultation with the Labour leaders.

What had happened? The idea of a sudden conversion of Sinn Féin deputies to a radical social-democratic programme was scarcely credible. In fact, contemporary personal records show an increasing interaction between Labour leaders and the Sinn Féin group organising the First Dáil. Labour – itself preparing to attend the Socialist International in Berne in spring 1919 – wanted a strong policy statement from the Dáil to offset its own lack of parliamentary representation in Ireland. Sinn Féin – intent on gaining the widest possible international recognition for the new state and its infant parliament – was prepared to accept a rhetorical endorsement of Labour policies. It had neither the means nor the intention of implementing them. It is impossible to read the detailed records of the time and not conclude – although, admittedly, the evidence is entirely circumstantial – that the 'Democratic Programme' was part of the price extracted by Labour leaders for withdrawing their candidates from the general election.

It may be doubted whether any such arrangement would have been entered into had such leaders as de Valera and Griffith been at liberty and in charge. Each would have recognised the risks of giving such ideological hostages to an uncertain future fortune.

Even without their direct involvement, other voices in Sinn Féin were raised against accepting a strongly-worded draft produced by the Labour leader, Tom Johnson.

On the eve of the First Dáil's inaugural meeting Michael Collins called a meeting of a small group of IRB members and presented drafts of the documents to be adopted by the Dáil.[4] The Declaration of Independence drew no comment; although PS O'Hegarty, who was present and records this IRB meeting, thought it long-winded. The Message to the Free Nations evoked the comment that it was a waste of time as the League would neither recognise Irish independence nor admit Ireland to the Peace Conference. The proposed 'Democratic Programme' gave rise to a lively debate with the preponderance of opinion going against it. According to O'Hegarty: 'It was urged that this declaration was in fact *ultra vires* for the Dáil, whose one and only business was to get the English out of Ireland, and that all internal and arguable questions like this should be left over until the English had actually been got out.'

Following a vote, Collins undertook to suppress the document but subsequently it was accepted that a somewhat more moderately phrased version, drawn up by Seán T O'Ceallaigh, would be presented. Thus, through a combination of secrecy, subterfuge, compromise and bargaining, the 'Democratic Programme' was ready to join the other three documents presented to the first session of the First Dáil for ratification. It was, in essence, a propaganda card played in a high-stake game of international recognition.

Much the same could be said for two of the other declaratory documents adopted. The Declaration of Independence, read out in turn in Irish, French and English, while the deputies stood in their places, recapitulated the analysis and re-affirmed the assertions of the Easter Proclamation of 1916. It ratified the Irish Republic proclaimed outside the GPO but tied it to a firmly democratic mandate — 'at the threshold of a new era in history the Irish electorate has in the General Election of December, 1918, seized the first occasion to declare by an overwhelming majority its firm allegiance to the Irish Republic.' And the Declaration ordained that:

... the elected Representatives of the Irish people alone have power to make laws binding on the people of Ireland, and the Irish Parliament is the only parliament to which the people will give its allegiance.

Thus, ironically by way of a British general election, on a franchise created by a British statute, Pearse's dream of the sovereign people was translated into parliamentary reality.

Similarly, the Message to the Free Nations of the World asserted Ireland's claim to be represented at the Versailles peace conference. It invoked Woodrow Wilson's own principles to claim the national right of self-determination and called 'upon every free nation to uphold her national claim to complete independence as an Irish Republic.' It was an appeal that fell on deaf ears in the great chancelleries of Europe.

Set beside the high rhetoric of these other documents, the bare and arid language of the Constitution presented to the Dáil attracted little attention. Alone among the documents of the day it was presented only in Irish (although subsequently a somewhat defective English version was supplied to the press). Its promoters made few claims for the Constitution. It was, said Seán T O'Ceallaigh, a provisional document containing just what was needed for the present; there would be need later to expand its provisions and it was open to any deputy in the future to propose amendments.

This almost dismissive presentation did less than justice to the Constitution presented to, and adopted by, the First Dáil. It was, after all, the first fundamental law of modern Ireland. It was to remain the basis of the Irish state until the adoption of the Irish Free State Constitution in 1922. It was a major link in the chain of

Irish political and institutional development as the country passed from colonial dependency to national independence. The Constitution is also a critical tool in understanding the nature of that process and an important corrective to the high-flown rhetoric of the Declaration of Independence and the radical scenario sketched out in the 'Democratic Programme.'

The five short articles of the Dáil Constitution of 1919 promise no revolution. Instead they incorporate, in a basic but clearly discernible form, the main elements of the British cabinet system of government. Thus, there is an elected Dáil which has full legislative power; the Irish phrase 'iomlán comhachta chun dlighthe dheunamh' is a perfect expression of the British doctrine of parliamentary sovereignty: a plenitude of legislative power untrammelled by any constraints of a written and rigid Constitution, let alone by any claims of judicial review.

Article 2 provides that all executive power is vested in a ministry chosen by the Dáil from among its own members and answerable to it. Here again, the separation of powers favoured in so many democratic systems is jettisoned in favour of Cabinet which, in Bagehot's classic description of the British Cabinet, is a buckle that fastens, a hyphen that joins, the legislative and executive arms of government in a single institution.

Article 3 provides for an elected Ceann Comhairle to preside over the Dáil. The Standing Orders provided were entirely based on British practice and the rulings of the chair stayed as firmly committed to Erskine May as any Mr Speaker at Westminster.

Article 4 reserved the money power to the Dáil and provided for regular audit. Article 5 laid down that this was a provisional constitution liable to amendment 'upon seven days written notice of motion for that specific purpose.' No particular procedure was required. The Dáil Constitution was entirely flexible and could be – and was – changed like any other act of parliament.

It is impossible to examine this first modern Irish Constitution and not notice its remarkable fidelity to the contemporary British model. Perhaps that should not surprise us. The British had remodelled their own governmental system under the pressures of the First World War. That cabinet system was seen to offer a government that was at once representative and responsible, effective and democratic. Moreover, the men who drafted the Dáil Constitution were familiar with the Westminster system; Ireland had not merely been a close witness but an actual and active participant in the evolution of modern British democracy. It was perhaps natural to copy the familiar mode of government rather than attempt any adventurous experiments with political institutions.

Yet the circumstances of Ireland in 1919 bore little resemblance to the political culture that nourished Westminster. The long-term legitimacy that shored up British institutions was not available to a Dáil that was technically an illegal assembly. The abstention of Unionists – and who could expect them to take up the Sinn Féin invitation to participate – meant that the Dáil was a one-party assembly.

This provoked the only serious attempt to reform procedures.[5] The suggestion was made, on a motion by J J Walsh, seconded by Seán MacEntee (both subsequently ministers in Irish governments): 'to bring the Constitution into harmony with the American idea of Committees elected by the whole House and clothed with similar powers.'

The course of the debate was instructive. Walsh argued that advisory, consultative committees were of no value since 'it rested with the responsible Minister to accept or reject their findings.' MacEntee said that 'under present circumstances there could be no real opposition to the Ministry.'

Collins replied that deputies had not bothered to attend committees and commented that 'it was news to him to hear that the members had no redress if they disapproved of the actions of the Ministry. The Dáil had absolute power to remove any

Minister.' There was a certain *ad hominem* quality about this response. Griffith, who was Acting President of the Ministry during de Valera's absence in the United States, was more direct in rejecting the committee proposal: 'the motion meant a complete revolution of the Constitution of Dáil Éireann. It meant taking away the responsibility of the Ministers and placing it in the hands of Committees. The suggestion that President de Valera was in favour of this departure was unfounded..... [the Constitution] might be adapted in normal times but under present circumstances it would be hopeless to try to function through Committees.'

Eoin MacNeill also opposed: 'It was a very revolutionary proposal and he did not believe that the country would approve it.' His amendment postponing the motion for twelve months was carried thirty-three to one.

The cautious and conservative approach to structures and procedures was also reflected in the laws made by the Dáil.[6] The Dáil legislated by decree but there was little distinction made between 'decrees', 'bills', 'ministerial orders' and even 'acts'. A full check-list is difficult to authenticate. These confusions are understandable given the disturbed circumstances of a Dáil operating infrequently and 'on the run'. But the broad thrust of legislative development is evident enough.

Between January 1919 and May 1921, the First Dáil held a total of twenty-one meetings and passed thirty-six decrees. The Second Dáil, which met on thirty-nine sitting days between August 1921 and June 1922 was mainly engaged in the political debate on the Treaty and passed only eight decrees. While some decrees had a clear and broadly applicable purpose, others were either inoperative or of little more than administrative convenience. Yet, a certain normalisation is evident over time in the case of the First Dáil. Early decrees were the products of Sinn Féin party policy outlined in the programme for national reconstruction. Later decrees emerged from the needs of the embryonic regime as it tried to 'build a polity within a polity' and cope with the tasks of administration. Thus, its first decree was the Declaration of Independence, its last the results of representations by Irish manufacturing interests to secure a protective policy.

In between, four decrees dealing with agriculture provided a Land Fund, encouraged afforestation and fishing, and established a Land Commission which reflected the influence of the original Sinn Féin programme. At the same time the Dáil Cabinet records show that the decree creating a Land Commission was thoroughly discussed and amended in Cabinet; the text was far more elaborate than earlier decrees.

Another 'agricultural' decree reflected a far wider determination to maintain order and the *status quo*. This was Decree 6 of 1920 relating to 'Claims on Land'. It was designed to protect occupiers of 'dairy, agricultural and residential holdings' from land-grabbing. In proposing the decree, the Minister for Home Affairs, Austin Stack *'explained that the people who were putting forward these claims were not nationalists at all. They were merely out to create a state of anarchy which ought to be put a stop to.'*[7] That task was left to what the decree called 'the forces of the Republic' (that is, the IRA).

This was only one example of the relationship between civil and military authority dealt with in a later essay in this volume. Other decrees covered the creation of Dáil courts and the operation of a remarkably well developed system of local government. Again these are dealt with in later essays. At this stage it is sufficient to note the extent to which the First Dáil, in its constitutional documents and its decrees, was intent on normalising and institutionalising its takeover of administration. It was all a long way from the dramatic social change that was promised in the 'Democratic Programme'.[8] There was going to be no revolution in the new Ireland. That judgement is well exemplified in the story of what happened to the high expectations of those women activists who had made their own distinctive contribution to the Irish struggle for independence. That is the theme of the next essay by Professor Maryann Valiulis.

Notes

1. The text, together with the Johnson draft discussed below is reproduced in Appendix 2b and 2c.

2. For a fuller discussion, with references, of relations between Labour and Sinn Féin see Brian Farrell, *'Labour and the Political Revolution'* in Donal Nevin, ed. *Trade Union Century*, Mercury Press, Cork 1994.

3. National Library of Ireland, Ms. 8556/20, Healy to O'Brien, 3 September 1918. O'Brien's later reaction quoted below in Ms. 8556/22, O'Brien to Healy, 6 November 1918.

4. PS O'Hegarty, *A History of Ireland under the Union, 1801 to 1922*, Methuen, London 1952, p.727 is the authority for this paragraph.

5. Dáil Éireann, *Minutes of Proceedings of the First Parliament of the Republic of Ireland*, Stationery Office, Dublin n.d. following based on minutes of session 17 September 1920, pp. 213-4.

6. For a check-list of Dáil decrees and discussion see Brian Farrell, 'The Legislation of a "Revolutionary" Assembly: Dáil Decrees, 1919-1922', *Irish Jurist*, X, 1975, pp.112-127.

7. Dáil Éireann, *Minutes First Dáil*, p.179.

8. Cf Patrick Lynch, *'The Social Revolution that never was'*, in Desmond Williams, ed., *The Irish Struggle, 1916-1922*, Routledge and Kegan Paul, London 1966.

See Appendix 2 p. xxx for The Constitution, Articles 1-5; The Democratic Programme of the First Dáil; The Johnson Draft of the Democratic Programme; Declaration of Independence; Message to the Free Nations of the World; Check-list of Dáil Decrees 1919-1922.

6

'Free Women in a Free Nation':
Nationalist Feminist Expectations for Independence
Maryann Gialanella Valiulis

Dr Maryann Gialanella Valiulis is a specialist in modern Irish history. She is the author of *Almost A Rebellion: The Irish Army Mutiny of 1924* and the award winning *Portrait of a revolutionary: General Richard Mulcahy and the Founding of the Irish Free State.* She is currently completing a study of the re-construction of gender ideology in the Irish Free State. Dr Valiulis is a lecturer in Women's Studies and Academic Coordinator of the Centre for Women's Studies at Trinity College.

◆◆◆◆◆◆◆◆◆◆

In the early years of the 20th Century, nationalist, feminist women had great expectations for independence. In the many and varied organisations which dotted the Irish cultural and intellectual landscape, women raised their voices and articulated their particular dreams for Ireland. Nationalist, suffragist, Home Ruler, socialist, all types of women were asking questions about gender relations in the future state.

Inghinidhe na hÉireann, the daughters of Éireann, was one such group. Militant, nationalist and feminist, their dream was of an independent Ireland in which women would be both free and equal. In their vision of the new state, women would not be bound 'by the frying pan and the fashion plate.' But rather, having proven their worth as comrades in a revolutionary struggle, women would fully participate in the political life of the state, in creating a new world.

Inghinidhe's origin is well-known.[1] The women – women like Maud Gonne, for example – who went on to found the Daughters of Éireann first came together in an effort to demonstrate that Ireland was not a loyal and contented part of the British Empire. The specific occasion was the visit of Queen Victoria to Dublin. Those loyal to the Queen were organising events in her honour – including a special event for children. The future members of Inghinidhe organised a counter-fête for nationalist children and thousands of youngsters were filled with jam buns and nationalist sentiments in this celebration of Irish nationalism.

Inghinidhe na hÉireann emerged from that event. The Daughters of Éireann went on to heighten the feminist consciousness of nationalist Ireland. Inghinidhe na hÉireann was part of a relatively small group of intellectuals who quite self-consciously attempted to define the cultural, intellectual and social parameters of the new state. They were an integral part of the cultural and intellectual re-vitalisation of Irish life. They were involved in the Abbey Theatre, in Sinn Féin and in the Labour movement. Always and everywhere, they put forward the case for women's involvement in the nationalist movement.

The women of Inghinidhe na hÉireann were a vibrant, self-confident group who challenged the *status quo* both in terms of nationalist and feminist ideology. Their importance lay not in terms of their numbers or even in terms of their actual activities. Their particular significance emerged from their ideology, from their attitude, from their stance in joining together militant nationalism and feminism. Indeed, it would be Inghinidhe's particular contribution that it challenged the traditional definition of 'nationalist woman' by imagining a community in which feminism and nationalism neither conflicted nor competed, but rather co-existed in harmony. Their existence opened up new possibilities for women, new definitions for womanhood.[2]

Central to the belief of the Daughters of Éireann was the view that nationalist women should – indeed must – play an active part in the upcoming struggle for independence, must assume a prominent role in the political process. What was necessary was 'to awaken Irishwomen to their responsibilities and long neglected duties' and to raise the position of women in the social and political life of the country.[3]

The Daughters of Éireann described themselves as feminists, talked of the feminist cause.[4] They had no doubt that women had a right to participate in the public life of the country – in the struggle for independence, in political discussions, in policy decisions. To all who would listen, they proclaimed their belief in women's innate equality, in her inherent right as [a] loyal citizen ... to participate in the body politic.[5]

Not only did women have a right to a place in the public arena, the Daughters of Éireann believed that there would be clear advantages which would accrue to Ireland if women participated in the political life of the country:

'It is not our intention to countenance any sex antagonism between Irish women and Irish men. ...but we think that men would be the better for a little of women's unselfishness and spirituality, and we look for the advent of women into public life for a lofty idealism and a purer atmosphere.'[6]

The Daughters of Éireann recognised, however, that there were difficulties to be overcome before women could raise the public life of the country. Like the suffragists, they recognised that women suffered from political disabilities, most notably the lack of the parliamentary franchise, the 'vote'. Unlike the suffragists, however, the Daughters of Éireann saw the solution to this problem in national terms - when Ireland was free, women would be free. Their goal was 'Free Women in a Free Nation.' 'It is not,' the Daughters of Éireann proclaimed, 'a question of putting Nationality before sex, or sex before Nationality ... The Feminist Cause in Ireland is best served by ignoring England and English politicians.'[7]

Thus the Daughters of Éireann would not countenance asking or even agitating for the vote from a foreign body:

'As our country has had her Freedom and her Nationhood taken from her by England, so also our sex is denied emancipation and citizenship by the same enemy. So therefore the first step on the road to freedom is to realise ourselves as Irishwomen – not only as Irish or merely as women, but as Irishwomen doubly enslaved and with a double battle to fight'.[8]

In this double battle, the Daughters of Éireann saw Irishmen as their allies. In a free Ireland, women would have political equality because they believed that Irishmen would never deny women their rightful place in the nation:

'...We feel sure that if the case were put logically and forcibly before our countrymen their love of freedom and sense of justice would compel them to give to women a voice and a place in the government of their country'.[9]

Having experienced oppression themselves, the leaders of a free Irish state would never subject women to such treatment. The Daughters of Éireann proclaimed that:

'...the men of Ireland, who have never countenanced the enslavery of other nations by the Anglo-Saxon, will [not] lower the standard of liberty and join with their enemies to enslave a sex. No. The men of our race, descended like us, from a long line of martyrs in the cause of liberty, will not try to keep our rights and our duties from us, and the day that Ireland stands free before the world shall see our emancipation too'.[10]

Subsequent events would demonstrate how foolhardy this assumption was.

But at the time, it did not seem to be an unfounded assumption. The nationalist organisations which the women of Inghinidhe na hÉireann would be associated with – organisations like Sinn Féin and the Gaelic League – did indeed seem to ascribe to the equality of women. The Gaelic League, for example, was 'the first Irish national society which accepted women as members on the same terms as men.'[11] And Sinn Féin was 'the first political party in these islands to accept women as full members' with women prominent on its Executive.[12] Indeed it was the members of the Daughters of Éireann who supplied the bulk of the recruits.[13]

In addition, some of their more prominent male colleagues seemed to support their aspirations. Arthur Griffith advocated votes for women. James Connolly dreamed of a new world order in which both class and gender hierarchies would be abolished. It seemed obvious to the Daughters of Éireann where nationalist, feminist women belonged:

'Women are denied a place in some of the most important political organisations in Ireland. The United Irish League (with the exception of one branch, we believe), the Loyal Orange Association, the Liberal Home Rule Association, are exclusively masculine bodies. The Gaelic League and the Sinn Féin Organisation are the only ones in existence at present where women are on an equal footing with men.[14]

Thus, it made sense for the members of Inghinidhe na hÉireann to trust that in the type of Ireland they envisioned, women would take their rightful place as equal members of society.

To those who remained sceptical, the Daughters of Éireann further argued that if women participated in the national movement they would demonstrate to Irish men their fitness for, and their worthiness to be entrusted with, a public role in the new state. By joining with their male colleagues in the revolutionary struggle, women would thus demonstrate the irrationality of the prejudice against them. Women could, through their example, convince men that women's exclusion from the public sphere was based simply on ignorance and prejudice – both of which would fall away as women proved themselves as worthy colleagues.[15]

There were, of course, warning signs that all would not be as easy or as simple as the Daughters of Éireann believed, that advanced nationalist views did not necessarily mean an enlightened outlook on women's issues. Hanna Sheehy

Skeffington, noted feminist and suffragist, filled the pages of *Bean na hÉireann* – the newspaper of the Daughters of Éireann – with caveats about trusting in the emancipated attitudes of the men of Sinn Féin and the Gaelic League. Some of these men, she contended, had not yet 'rounded Cape Turk where women are concerned.'[16] It was a prophetic critique.

Contained within Inghinidhe na hÉireann's forthright demand for independence and equality, was a challenge to the more traditional aspects of women's role in society and a rejection of the notion of separate spheres, of the idea that women's activities should be confined to the domestic arena, while men inhabited the public world. Their message was simple. Domesticity was boring. Domesticity was stifling. Domesticity did nothing to further either women's growth and development or the freedom of Ireland.

But Inghinidhe na hÉireann saw a solution to the drudgery of domesticity, to the confines of traditional married life: political equality. Once women assumed their rightful role as comrades, once they were admitted into 'the equal rights of citizenship,' the narrowness and isolation of traditional married life would disappear.[17] As true comrades and equals, men and women, husbands and wives, would work together to build a new Ireland.

This rejection of the idea of separate spheres, of the domestic realm as women's natural habitat and Inghinidhe na hÉireann's insistence on women's right to be considered as citizens was important in establishing an alternative model of womanhood for nationalist feminist women. The Daughters of Éireann delineated a wider definition of what was appropriate for women – more than that, what it was women's obligation to do – for the nationalist movement. Their gender ideology expanded women's role into the public sphere where women would work as partners with men in the broader political scene. Woman as citizen was their ideal.

The overtly feminist attitude characteristic of Inghinidhe na hÉireann did not survive them. Their legacy was important, however. Their vision of an Ireland, free and equal, equal and free, was one which would remain the goal of women's groups throughout the early years of independence.

Inghinidhe na hÉireann did not live long enough to witness the tumultuous years of the Irish revolutionary period, 1916-1922. The organisation was absorbed, *en masse*, into a new woman's organisation, Cumann na mBan.

Cumann na mBan was the woman's auxiliary of the Irish Volunteers, founded to 'organise Irish women to advance the cause of Irish freedom.' Among its founding members were many of the wives or relatives of the leading figures of the Volunteer movement. Although confident in their belief that their organisation was vital to the independence struggle, they saw themselves as helpmates. The founding meeting set the tone, declaring that the political arena was to be reserved for men, while women's role was to 'put Ireland first,' by helping to arm the men.[18]

Cumann na mBan members played an active and important role in the 1916 Rising. During Easter Week, in the confusion generated by orders and counterorders, mishaps and miscalculations, the work of the women of Cumann na mBan was vital. They acted as messengers as the leaders of the Rising sought to bring a semblance of order to the chaos of Easter Monday. They commandeered vans, arranged for provisions and organised to have food and ammunition brought through the British cordon.[19] Their services were critical in allowing the Volunteers to continue to fight against the numerically superior British forces for almost a week.

The Easter Rising had a profound effect on nationalist women. On an ideological level, the Proclamation of the Republic was important in validating nationalist and feminist expectations for equality in the new state and for demonstrating the tranformative potential of the struggle for independence. The Proclamation of the Republic was addressed to both Irishmen and Irishwomen and promised equal rights and equal opportunities for all of its citizens. Indeed the Proclamation of the Republic seemed to vindicate Inghinidhe na hÉireann's belief that women would be equal in a free Ireland.

The Proclamation of the Republic, moreover, legitimated women's role in the new state and gave formal recognition to their place in the nationalist movement. Coupled with the participation of Cumann na mBan members in the events of Easter week, the Proclamation strengthened the 'feminist impulse' within Cumann na mBan[20] and fuelled their desire to 'assert their right as citizens.'[21]

After the Rising, after the executions and the mass arrests, it fell to the women to pick up the pieces of the now tattered revolutionary movement – which they did, and did well.

It was the women, under the leadership of Kathleen Clark, who operated the Volunteers' Dependent Fund which not only provided relief, but served to keep the nationalist movement together. It gave nationalists a focus and a purpose as they began to regroup after 1916.

It was also the women who were responsible for the propaganda which helped mould popular opinion in favour of those who were now being called the martyrs of 1916. They organised a remembrance crusade – pictures and postcards, masses, publication of the prose and poetry of the dead leaders. The women not only ensured that the leaders of 1916 would be remembered, they raised the revolutionary fervour of nationalist Ireland. Such was their zeal that the British military commander was forced to admit to his Prime Minister that there was a strong resurgence of feeling for the revolutionaries and that it was due primarily to the actions and speeches of 'young priests and militant women.'[22]

The women of Cumann na mBan believed that their participation in 1916 and in the leadership of the subsequent remembrance crusade earned them the right to be treated as free and equal citizens. In a declaration in 1917, they stated:

'Cumann na mBan is proud that its members rallied under the Republican Flag in Easter Week, 1916, and claim that by taking their places in the firing line and in every other way helping in the establishment of the Irish Republic, they regained for the women of Ireland the rights that belonged to them under the old Gaelic civilisation where women were free to devote to the service of their country every talent and capacity with which they were endowed; which rights were guaranteed to them in the Republican Proclamation of Easter Week.'[23]

Thus, when the Volunteers returned home and the political and military struggle for independence increased in intensity, women had a 'larger, more active, less subordinate, and more consciously feminist organisation.'[24]

At the end of World War I, the British parliament granted the Parliamentary franchise to all women over thirty years of age. The 1918 election gave women their first opportunity to use their newly acquired political power. Sinn Féin actively courted the newly enfranchised women, promising that 'as in the past, so in the future the womenfolk of the Gael shall have high place in the Councils of a freed Gaelic nation.'[25] Sinn Féin also nominated two women, albeit only two, to stand for election. In Dublin, Constance Markievicz was elected the first woman to the House of Commons. Winifred Carey was defeated in Belfast. No women were nominated by the Irish Parliamentary Party.

Sinn Féin candidates, true to their election pledge, refused to take their seats in the House of Commons but rather in January, 1919, established the First Dáil. The Social and Democratic Programme followed the example of the 1916 Proclamation both in content and form. It was addressed to both men and women. It invoked the principles of Liberty, Equality and Justice, and affirmed 'the duty of every man and woman to give allegiance and service to the Commonwealth.'[26] Subsequent policy discussions envisioned a programme of social reform which explicitly mentioned equal pay for women and men doing the same work – a principle which would be rejected in 1935 – as well as protective legislation for women.[27]

Thus when women assumed their responsibilities in the guerrilla struggle for independence, they did so confident in the knowledge that they had a legitimate and important role to play as citizens of the Republic. They were vital to the success of the war of independence. Women were instrumental in putting Ireland's case for freedom before the world and blackening the reputation of the British government. They acted as couriers, bringing vital information to the fighting units of the IRA. In more traditional ways, they ministered to the sick, tended to the wounded and performed those domestic chores which enabled the men of the IRA to carry on the struggle against the British. Their houses were raided during the middle of the night. They were terrorised by the British forces.[28] They themselves were arrested and imprisoned.

Despite the growing danger, nationalist women also continued to be politically active. They sat on municipal boards and county councils. For example, in 1920 there were five newly elected women on Dublin Corporation – Jennie Wyse Power, Hanna Sheehy Skeffington, Kathleen Clarke, Margaret McGarry and Anne E Ashton. Women served as Republican judges, implementing the law of the Dáil as the courts of the Irish Republic supplanted those of the British. Women, moreover, remained an active and visible part of the national executive of Sinn Féin. Through it all, women showed themselves fiercely determined to play their part in the struggle for independence with courage and bravery.

At the end of the Anglo-Irish war, there seems to have been a general recognition that women had played an admirable part in the independence struggle. Constance Markievicz, in her presidential address to the 1921 annual convention of Cumann na mBan, duly recognised the work of these women 'who stood in the gap of danger during the time of ... war,' who did 'daring and brave things' which history would applaud.[29]

Countess Markievicz's sentiments were echoed by Michael Collins, when he said: 'Few appreciate what Ireland owes to the women who stood their ground during the first few years and no thanks that anyone can bestow on them will be too great.'[30]

Cathal Brugha, Minister for Defence during the Anglo-Irish war, paid his tribute to women for 'keeping the spirit alive,' for keeping 'the flame alive and burning.'[31] In general, male nationalists applauded women's bravery, heralded their resistance to terror and recognised their essential contribution to the military struggle.

The praise and gratitude which women received for their part in the Anglo-Irish war changed, however, with the advent of the civil war. Cumann na mBan rejected the Treaty overwhelmingly – the first nationalist organisation to do so. The women deputies in the Dáil spoke passionately against the agreement and all six voted against it.

When civil war followed, once again women took up their role in the military struggle. Cumann na mBan rallied to the Republican cause. They gave of their time and energy. Perhaps, more significantly, they gave psychological support to the Republican cause. Women became the staunchest defenders of the Republic. They were seen as rigid and uncompromising, willing to shed more blood in pursuit of an ideal. For this, women were blamed for the civil war.

The pro-Treaty historian, PS O'Hegarty, for example, wrote that Dublin, during the civil war, was full of 'hysterical women,' who had been turned into 'unlovely, destructive-minded, arid begetters of violence' by the revolution.[32] In a very telling passage, O'Hegarty said:

'Left to himself, man is comparatively harmless. He will always exchange smokes and drinks and jokes with his enemy, and he will always pity the 'poor devil' and wish that the whole business was over... It is woman ... with her implacability, her bitterness, her hysteria, that makes a devil of him.'[33]

Women's hostility to the Treaty rebounded against them. Some, like O'Hegarty, blamed women for the divisiveness and violence which plagued the country, a position clearly not supported by the events of the period.[34] However, the civil war was such a devastating experience that the need to scapegoat, to blame was enormous. Women were one easy and obvious target. Thus, the civil war had a very clear, albeit negative effect, on male perception of women's right to participate in the political life of the country. This negative perception translated into legislation, into an effort on the part of successive Free State governments to define women out of politics. In fact, simply put, the Cosgrave and then the de Valera government sought to eliminate women from public life. Although the Constitution of 1921 gave women over the age of 21 the right to vote and hold office on terms of equality with men, and although there seemed to have been no question but that those who drafted the Constitution asserted the fundamental legal equality of men and women in terms of rights, duties and obligations, yet that equality was undermined by the government's subsequent gender legislation:

1. The Juries Acts of 1924 and 1927 which, for all practical purposes, barred women from serving on juries;
2. The 1925 Civil Service Act which restricted women's right to employment in the upper echelons of the Service.
3. The 1932 ban on employing married women teachers, a ban which eventually applied to the entire civil service;
4. The 1935 Conditions of Employment Act which gave the Minister for Industry and Commerce the right to restrict the number of women employed in any given industry;

5.   Finally, the 1937 Constitution explicitly assigned women
      the role of guardians of the hearth and family.

This legislation took away rights which women already
enjoyed and severely limited women's political and economic
freedom. The message was clear – women were to be restricted to
the domestic sphere, to be rendered publicly invisible.

The government justified this legislation by asserting that
women did not belong in the public sphere, that the primary role
of women was marriage and motherhood, that women's place was
in the home, tending to the needs of their husbands, raising their
children. As a corollary, the government also added that 'true Irish
women' had no desire to be wrenched from 'The bosoms of their
families, from their cherished household duties, from the
preparation of their husband's dinners.'[35]

Feminists disagreed. They insisted that women could inhabit
both the public and the domestic sphere, could be citizens as well
as wives and mothers. Feminists joined together to fight the
gender legislation of the 1920s and 1930s. They claimed their rights
under the Constitution, declaring that the government's gender
legislation violated that document. They countered the
government's assertions about natural roles by arguing that it was
women's right to serve in the public sphere and their obligation to
add their unique perspective to the political debate. Finally,
feminists pointedly reminded their male colleagues that through
their participation in the events of 1916-1922, they had earned
inclusion in the body politic on terms of equality with men. As
Senator Jennie Wyse Power eloquently said:

'No men in a fight for freedom ever had such loyal cooperation
from their women as the men who compose the present Executive
Council. When they wanted messengers to go into dangerous
places, they did not call on members of their own sex. When they

wanted auditors to go out when the old Local Government Board broke down it was women they sent. It was women inspectors that went round ... and did all the work for them in that terrible time ... and these are the people who tell us that we are physically unfit.'[36]

It seemed like betrayal.

The expectations which had run so high in the early years of the century, the confidence that once Ireland had achieved its freedom and independence, women would be freed from the political and economic inequalities which shackled them were obviously dashed. The government legislated, the Catholic Church sanctioned, and the press popularised a restrictive and diminutive view of women's role in the new state.

There were many reasons for the gender legislation of the 1920s and 1930s – the desire to restore traditional order and hierarchy, the need to consolidate power, to name but two. Significantly, however, a gendered definition of citizenship helped the government underline the conservative nature of the post-revolutionary state and announce that the tranformative potential of the revolution was simply not to be. The dreams of Inghinidhe na hÉireann would not be fulfilled in the reality of the Irish Free State.

Notes

1. For a detailed discussion of the origins and work of Inghinidhe na hÉireann, see Margaret Ward, *Unmanageable Revolutionaries*, Dingle, Co. Kerry, Brandon Books, 1983.
2. Margaret Ward, *Unmanageable Revolutionaries*, Dingle, Co. Kerry: Brandon Books, 1983, p.86.
3. *Bean na hÉireann*,Vol.1, #3, January, 1909.
4. *Bean na hÉireann*, Vol.1, #4, February, 1909.
5. *Bean na hÉireann*, Editorial, Vol.1, #3, January, 1909.
6. *Bean na hÉireann*,Editorial, Vol.1, #3, January, 1909.

7. *Bean na hÉireann*, Vol.1, #4, Feb., 1909.

8. *Bean na hÉireann*, Vol.1, #9, July, 1909.

9. *Bean na hÉireann*, February, 1909.

10. *Bean na hÉireann*, Vol.1, #3, January, 1909.

11. Brian Farrell, *Countess Markievicz and the Women of the Revolution*, in *Leaders and Men [sic] of the Easter Rising*, edited by F X Martin, Ithica, Cornell University Press 1967.

12. Marie O'Neill, *From Parnell to DeValera*, Blackwater Press, 1991, pp.57-62.

13. Margaret Ward, *Unmanageable Revolutionaries*, Kerry: Brandon Books, 1983, pp.66-67.

14. *Bean na hÉireann*, February, 1909.

15. *Bean na hÉireann*, Vol.1, #3, January, 1909.

16. *Bean na hÉireann*, No.13.

17. *Bean na hÉireann*, Vol.1, #3, January, 1909, Editorial reply.

18. Lil Conlon, *Cumann na mBan and the Women of Ireland*, Kilkenny: Kilkenny People Ltd., 1969

19. Margaret Ward, *Unmanageable Revolutionaries*, Kerry: Brandon Books, 1983, p.111. See Ward for a detailed account of the activities of the women of Cumann na mBan and the Irish Citizens' Army.

20. Brian Farrell, *Markievicz and the Women of the Revolution*, in *Leaders and Men of the Easter Rising*, ed. F X Martin, Ithica: Cornell University Press, 1967, p.236. Beth McKillen in her work on the relationship of Irish feminism to the separatist tradition agrees with Farrell and goes on to define the feminist impulse as 'an increasing political interest on the part of women in such peculiarly women's causes as women's suffrage, equal rights and pay for women and marriage and divorce reform.' Beth McKillen, *Irish Feminism and Nationalist Separatism, 1914-23. Éire Ireland*, Vol.XVII, No.3, p.65

21. Quoted in Beth McKillen, *Irish Feminism and Nationalist Separatism, Éire Ireland*, Vol.XVII, No.3, p.65.

22. Quoted in Anne Haverty, *Constance Markievicz - An Independent Life*, London: Pandora Press, 1988, p.166.

23. Quoted in Beth McKillen, *Irish Feminism and Nationalist Separatism, 1914-23, Éire Ireland*, Vol.XVII:No.3, p.66.

24. Beth McKillen, *Irish Feminism and Nationalist Separatism*, 1914-23, *Éire Ireland*, Vol.XVII:No.3, p.67.

25. Quoted in Diana Norman, *Terrible Beauty A Life of Constance Markievicz*, Dublin: Poolbeg Press, 1987, p.188.

26. Minutes of Proceedings of the First Parliament of the Republic of Ireland, 1919-1921, 21 January 1919, pp.22-23.

27. Minutes of Proceedings of the First Parliament of the Republic of Ireland, 10 April 1919, p.53

28. For a vivid description of the terrorising effect of these raids, see Kathleen Clarke, *Revolutionary Woman*, Dublin: The O'Brien Press, 1991.

29. Quoted in Lil Conlon, *Cumann na mBan and the Women of Ireland*, Kilkenny: Kilkenny People Ltd., 1969, p.238.

30. Quoted in Lil Conlon, *Cumann na mBan and the Women of Ireland* Kilkenny: People Press, 1969, pp.263-264.

31. Beth McKillen, *Irish Feminism and Nationalist Separatism, 1914-1923, Éire Ireland*, Vol.XVII:No.4, p.86.

32. Quoted in Brian Farrell, *Markievicz and the Women of the Revolution*, in *Leaders and Men of the Easter Rising: Dublin 1916* edited by F X Martin, New York: Cornell University Press,1967, p.227.

33. P S O'Hegarty, *The Victory of Sinn Féin*, Dublin: Talbot Press, Dublin, 1924, p.105.

34. For a detailed discussion of the negotiations and discussions which occurred in the months prior to the civil war, see *The Evolution of a Revolutionary: General Richard Mulcahy and the Founding of the Irish Free State*, Maryann Gialanella Valiulis. Kentucky: University Press of Kentucky, 1992.

35. Editorial in the *Dundalk Democrat* quoted in the *Irish Independent*, 14 February 1927.

36. *Senate Debates*, 17 December 1925, Vol.6, col.258-259.

7
The Courts of Dáil Éireann

Mary Kotsonouris

Mary Kotsonouris served as a Judge of the District Court for nine years and is Chairperson of the Sentence Review Group. She is the author of *Retreat from Revolution: The Dáil Courts, 1920-24* which was published on the 75th anniversary of the founding of Dáil Éireann. She is currently writing a book on the Dáil Courts Winding-up Commission for the Irish Legal History Society.

◆◆◆◆◆◆◆◆◆◆

The concept of creating a legal system corresponding with a revolutionary or subversive movement was not novel in 1919, nor even in 1906 when it formed part of the Sinn Féin programme at the National Convention held in the Mansion House. Daniel O'Connell had urged the setting-up of secessionist courts during the Repeal Agitation, and the Land League had its own courts to fix rents in the 1880s. While such an idea would be the ultimate *'non serviam'* to established authority, realistically it must have seemed that it would remain only an aspiration of the windy, and somewhat woolly, rhetoric of separatism. Surprisingly, it all came true. Not only was a separatist assembly established, as we have seen, but also a separate administration from the beginning. The first Minister for Home Affairs was Arthur Griffith, onlie-begetter of the theory that arbitration could and would replace the hierarchy of courts and adversarial trials whose fulcrum was the Bench and Bar. The minutes of Dáil Éireann show that he did not lose sight of this ideal which is a pervasive one (John Banville has explained the persistence of the Robin Hood legend as 'humankind's longing for goodness and justice beyond the iron shackles of the law'). In fact, colours were nailed to the mast by the Dáil decreeing that national arbitration courts were to be established in every county five days before the question of possible structures was even broached in the Ministry of Home Affairs. A committee, with Griffith in the chair, was set up and over another year, reports, schemes, suggestions and proposals were put forward, mulled over, amended and withdrawn. And, predictably enough, the Decree which established the courts of Dáil Éireann, twelve months later, bore little affinity to the system Griffith had sketched – with passion, if not precision – to the delegates in the Mansion House in 1906. However, at the same time, there occurred a sea-change in the administration of justice in Ireland which was a source of fascination and bewilderment to international observers. While the revolutionaries above in the Dáil fumbled about with their committees and reports, scheming to snatch the scales from blinded – and British – Justice, the people coolly went ahead and did it themselves.

There are two different strands in the phenomenon of communal devices for imposing law and order which first appeared to take shape around the summer of 1919. Indeed, a full two months before the Dáil passed the decree on arbitration, the *Clare Champion* reported that a meeting of the local Sinn Féin Comhairle Ceanntair in Ennis on 12 April 1919 had decided to set up arbitration courts to which disputes about land could be referred. This led to the West Clare Arbitration Courts which were regulated by a written constitution. Not only were there Parish Courts with three elected judges, but an appeal lay to a superior District Court of five judges. A skeletal provision for fines and the restriction of licensing hours went beyond the concept of submission to arbitration but set the pattern for the practice in future courts. Land agitation, in which there were uncomfortable elements of Whiteboyism, was increasingly evident in the West of Ireland in reports of cattle driving, destruction of property and vicious attacks on landowners. The possibility was strong that confident hopes for a new beginning, buoyed by the creation of an Irish parliament, would be drowned in the blood-red tide of atrocities. Yet the expectations of those who looked towards leaders to right the wrongs of the long-dispossessed could not be ignored. Sinn Féin, therefore, encouraged the growth of *ad hoc* tribunals which worked to find a compromise. They took some of the land from those who had, to give to those who had not, depending on the individual case and if a fair price could be worked out – the nucleus of the Land Commission, which, in fact, sprang directly from them. Within a very short time, it became a common practice to bring the claims of small holders to these hearings and for the landowners to be present or to be represented by a solicitor. The prosecutor in a Crimes Court at Ballinasloe alleged that it was an extremely bad case as the accused had refused to take the matter to the arbitration courts.[1] They were widely seen as making an effort to be fair in their conclusions and thus a strong factor in dampening down unrest and disorder'.[1]

As political violence grew and the police withdrew to the comparative safety of their barracks, the other element in keeping the peace was that local members of the Irish Volunteers organised themselves as village constables. They investigated robberies and assaults, recovered stolen property and administered swift punishment to wrongdoers. This frequently took the form of 'a good hiding', but also of public shame, such as being paraded through the streets before Sunday Mass. Banishment from the county, or the province, or sometimes from the country was a particularly harsh punishment. In the House of Commons, the Irish Attorney General was accused of turning a blind eye 'to the use of England as a sort of convict settlement for men deported by Sinn Féin' because he was secretly happy to have criminal types removed from his jurisdiction. Cahir Davitt was a young barrister beginning to have some success practising on the Connaught

Circuit. He recalled that in the spring of 1920 he had to endure the disappointment of cases, in which he had already been briefed, being removed from the jurisdiction of the County Court and the Assize Court to the Republican Courts and 'there disposed of without my assistance' as he ruefully put it. By that time, the two strands had merged and all types of disputes, as well as complaints of a criminal nature, were brought to the 'Sinn Féin or Republican Courts' whose proceedings were regularly reported in the provincial press. They also reported that the sittings of the County Courts and Petty Sessions were brief because litigants failed to appear. Jurymen refused the summons to duty and scores of Justices of the Peace resigned their commissions. The extraordinary show of civil disobedience was the subject of much comment in England and elsewhere. Andy Cope, the Assistant Under-Secretary at Dublin Castle, warned the British Cabinet that the courts were doing more harm to the prestige of their government than all the assassinations. In May 1920, Austin Stack, who was now the Minister for Home Affairs, finally circularised the Sinn Féin Clubs with the details of a scheme for the organisation of arbitration courts which was closely modelled on those in West Clare. Public meetings were held to elect District Judges. Newspapers gave prominence to the first sittings of the District Arbitration Courts, the judges' names and detailed accounts of the cases heard, all with an air of suppressed excitement. In the meantime, these courts had already been superseded, in theory at least, by the Decree which Dáil Éireann passed on 29 June 1920 to establish Courts of Justice and Equity and to empower the Ministry (of Home Affairs) to establish courts having a Criminal Jurisdiction. It is important to stress, however, that the authorisation to set up what might be called a proper system of courts with coercive jurisdiction did not affect those courts which continued throughout the summer of 1920 and that another year was to pass before the Ministry was in a position to exercise effective control over them.

In the *Constructive Work of Dáil Éireann Part 1* – the first of an incomplete series written by Erskine Childers to publicise the successes of its administration and published in 1921 – the regulations for the operation of the National Arbitration Courts are set out. All parties were to sign a submission to abide by the decision of the court and not to re-submit the claim to an 'enemy tribunal'. In his historical summary, Childers noted that the West Clare scheme had already been in operation but makes no mention of autonomous courts active in other places; an understandable omission, given that the purpose of the publication was to attribute all the achievement to the Dáil's initiative. In any event, the gathering of these disparate tribunals under the national assembly seemed to bless their efforts so far. Childers does not attempt to reconcile the successful criminal prosecutions, which he lists, to the absence of any such jurisdiction within the ambit of arbitration. Instead, he sees the progression as one from informal methods to the inevitable development of 'vesting the courts to enforce their decrees and compel the attendances of parties and witnesses'. His claim that the new system sanctioned by the Decree of 29 June 1920 was in full operation by September is somewhat weakened by Cahir Davitt's recollection that he and his fellow judges were only settling the details of the Constitution and Rules in that month. It is more likely that the Home Affairs Ministry had been able to give merely preliminary instructions to court officials before conditions worsened and 'war was declared on the courts', in the words of Childers. The true position is obscured by the loss of the Ministry's own records for this period during a raid on its offices in December 1920. When Davitt went south in November, Stack told him that no arrangements could be made by his office. All he could supply were the names of some of the Registrars, with whom the Circuit Judge would have to make contact as best he could – without putting his alias in too much jeopardy! The correspondence files of the Ministry reveal that contact with the Registrars was reopened as early as May 1921; court fees and deposits, collected over the previous six months, were accounted for and paid over. The submission of individual courts to the authority of Dáil Éireann was never questioned.[2]

The Constitution and Rules of the new courts appeared in a booklet which was always referred to as '*The Judiciary*' and was not in circulation until after the Truce. A Supreme Court was established which had unlimited jurisdiction. At the lower end there was a court in every parish with three elected justices. Each parliamentary constituency had a District Court with five judges elected by all the parish justices in that area. There would be three circuit sittings every year of the District Court presided over by a professional judge in which civil cases involving more than £100 in value would be heard as well as serious criminal charges. The limit in the Parish Courts was £10. The President of the Supreme Court was James Creed Meredith K C, Professor Arthur Clery of University College, Dublin, Diarmuid Crowley and Cahir Davitt were the other professional judges; all were barristers and they were paid £750 per annum from August 1920. Although Davitt and Crowley were appointed as Circuit Judges, they were often required to sit with the bench in the Supreme Court and, later, both Meredith and Clery took circuit sittings. Plans for the operation of the new scheme were thrown into disarray by a change in the attitude of the authorities towards the Sinn Féin courts. From mid-July onwards, arbitration courts up and down the country were raided by armed police and the military. Books and papers were destroyed or confiscated and officials arrested. In one such raid on 12 August 1920, the President of the Cork District Court, Terence McSwiney, was arrested; he was to die on hunger strike seventy-four days later. As martial law tightened its grip on successive counties, the courts were forced underground. With commendable courage, Davitt and Crowley set out in October to see if it were possible to organise circuit sittings, Davitt to Munster and Crowley to the West. The latter was arrested at his second sitting when he refused to disperse the court in the middle of a raid; he was court-martialled and imprisoned for thirteen months. Cahir Davitt, the much younger man with the cooler head - he was only twenty-six – managed to hold courts, in cunning, secrecy and danger, in the counties of Cork, Limerick, Kerry, Clare and Longford. In between, he slipped back to Dublin for other courts; incredibly, one court was held under the guise of a professional consultation in the Four Courts, the heart of the judicial establishment! That the courts, particularly in Munster, survived the dark days of 'The Terror' is clear not only from the reports of Registrars, but also from the fact that they were up and running at least two months before the Truce.

With the hostilities over and communication once again possible, Stack lost no time in bringing the courts under the centralised control of his Ministry. Directions on the election of Judges, the form of the regular reports and the return of court fees were sent out, as well as a team of organisers to supervise the whole operation and report back to him.[3] Davitt saw a great expansion in the work of the Dáil Courts over this time, although there were some half-hearted raids by the RIC and complaints to the Liaison Officers on both sides. In spite of the Treaty which supposed that the former courts would be rehabilitated or, at least, supported until the Free State came into existence, the Dáil judicial system still held centre stage. All criminal trials outside Dublin took place at Circuit Courts with juries and the State gaols opened to receive their prisoners. Local authorities sued for rates and prosecuted breaches of bye-laws in parish courts. Although an Assistant Minister for Home Affairs directed their administration ostensibly under the authority of Dáil Éireann, he had been appointed by the Provisional Government. The so-called 'British' courts barely functioned in the country, and in the city of Dublin it appears there was ample work for both jurisdictions. Questions were once again raised by the House of Commons but Churchill obviously felt there were more urgent things to worry about in the Irish situation. The matter was only mentioned twice at meetings of the Provisional Government.'

Even at this remove, it is difficult to gauge the attitude of the Provisional Government towards the Dáil Courts, which blossomed under its 'benevolent neutrality'. When the Proclamation, which announced that the Government had entered upon its functions under the terms of the Treaty, was issued 16 January 1922, it also announced, *inter alia*, that the courts of the former British administration were to continue as before. There was a storm of protest, but George Nicholls, as Assistant Minister for Home Affairs, reassured the faithful that this announcement had nothing to do with the Dáil Courts which were the only legal courts of the Irish people. Moreover, he urged that 'all necessary steps must be taken to boycott the Enemy Courts until the Irish people approve of the Free State Government.'

It was an extraordinary directive to be given by a government minister two days after the Proclamation but it was merely a precursor of the schizophrenia that disabled any hope of a realistic policy where the administration of justice was concerned. Dan Browne, a solicitor, who had administered the Dáil Courts from their establishment, left in March to work for de Valera in the coming elections. The Minister, Eamonn Duggan, upbraided him for his dereliction of this vital work although the Law Officer was then advising the Government that the Dáil Courts should be wound up without delay. On the few occasions that the matter of dual jurisdiction was raised in cabinet, it was postponed for further discussion. Not only was no effort made to show public support for the established courts, in line with the sentiments of the Proclamation, but the stream of complaints, from Resident Magistrates and County Judges, that they were obstructed from carrying out their duties, was consistently ignored.

With the destruction of the Four Courts and the outbreak of civil war, there was an abrupt change of policy. Three of the judges were out on circuit when telegrams were dispatched informing them that the 'Cabinet of Dáil Éireann' had ordered the cessation of the circuits and they were to return to Dublin. Two days later, 13 July 1922, James Creed Meredith sat to hear routine *ex parte* applications: he read from a letter which, remarkably, was addressed to Cahir Davitt, a Circuit Judge, to the effect that the Dáil Éireann Cabinet had decided that there should be no further sittings of the Supreme Court. The order was to be complied with at once. In fact the decision had been taken by the Provisional Government three days previously. What had not, apparently, been taken into account was the inherent power of judges to hear certain matters, in or out of court. A military prisoner, George Plunkett, lately captured at the surrender of the Four Courts, applied for and was granted a conditional order of *habeas corpus* by Judge Crowley. For reasons that remain unfathomable, the Government chose to make this single case into a *cause célèbre*.

The order, in the usual form, directed the Minister for Defence and the Governor of Mountjoy to show cause for the prisoner's detention, which was not difficult. It had already been publicly announced that he and others like him would be treated as military captives and given privileges not accorded to ordinary prisoners. The most junior barrister could have drafted the replying affidavit that a state of emergency existed and that the matter was outside the civil powers. Instead, on 24 July, the evening before the adjourned hearing, the Cabinet, again in the name of the non-functioning Dáil Éireann, rescinded the decree of 29 June 1920, which had established the courts. Professor Farrell has pointed out that this was the only Dáil Decree to have been rescinded; it was too drastic a step to take if all its purpose was to thwart an individual rebel. One immediate effect was that George Gavan Duffy, Minister for Foreign Affairs, and later President of the High Court, resigned in protest. Crowley, not a judge to take the easy way out like Solomon or Pontius Pilate, sat the next day, made the *habeas corpus* order absolute and ordered the arrest of General Mulcahy, the Minister for Defence, because he had failed to appear. He was to suffer for his judicial insolence; he was plucked off O'Connell Street three weeks later and thrown into jail without trial – his second spell of incarceration for acting as a Dáil Judge! Many voices were raised, including that of Darrell Figgis, to say that the ending of the courts was a matter for Dáil Éireann which had set them up in the first place and it should be left to the Dáil when it reconvened. County Councils passed resolutions of protest.

The recall of the judges from circuit, the suppression of the Supreme Court and the erasure of the instrument creating them all took place within a span of two weeks. Not only was this done without putting alternative courts in a state of readiness, it was done without any effort to prepare the public for the upheaval.

When the Government made an announcement to the public about the closing-down of the courts, which its members had themselves created, it stressed that there was a perfectly sound legal system already in place for years. It had far more facilities than the Dáil Courts had, and experienced personnel, all under the authority of native government, and for which the taxpayer was paying. It was foolish and wasteful to continue financing two opposing judicial systems, especially when the new one lacked so much embellishment. Everything in the statement was self-evidently true. No one seems to have commented that it was all equally true during the previous six months when the same government had chosen to ignore the claims of these grand courts and given its real, if tacit, support to the inadequate ones. What had suddenly changed its view?

Until papers turn up in which some contemporary observer provides a shrewd analysis, we are left to guess the motive for what Gavan Duffy rightly characterised as 'a panic stricken decision'. There is no evidence of British pressure. Churchill watched the manoeuvrings of the Provisional Government like an alert Guardian Angel, but his vigilance regarding legal matters seems to have been concentrated on urging that the Republicans be dislodged from the Four Courts – in a purely physical sense. Hugh Kennedy, the Law-Officer, had advised on transferring the functions of the Dáil Courts to rejuvenated petty Sessions and County Courts, but that was months before and nothing had been done. Of course, it must not be forgotten that the sands of time were running out on both sets of courts, and the more the problem was left on the long finger, the nearer the solution. Ideally, once the implementation of the Treaty terms were agreed, an election for a constituent assembly would be held, whose primary purpose was to approve a constitution to create the Irish Free State. The establishment of wholly new courts for independent Ireland would wipe the jurisdictional slate clean of outmoded tags – 'Republican' as well as 'British'. The split over the Treaty threw the whole timetable out of kilter. The publication of the draft constitution and the election did not happen until 6 June 1922: the Civil War broke out within weeks. The new Dáil did not meet until September and the Constitution of the Irish Free State was passed on 6 December. It was another year and a half before the new judicial system was established. However, this latter delay was not, and could not have been, foreseen in July 1922.

It may have appeared as a practical step to demonstrate that there would be no further attempt to accommodate Republican nostalgia now that the Four Courts had been cleared of its garrison. Although there had never been 'anything of a political tendency to hamper the operation of the courts' as one Limerick parish clerk protested, it was hardly hoped that there would be no change in that respect. Perhaps it was felt desirable to anticipate partisanship by depriving it of a forum. If that were the motive, why did the Government not say so? Certainly none of the many protesters made the connection between the suppression of the courts and the outbreak of civil war. What they expressed was bewilderment at the sudden change in policy and anger because the courts, which they had been taught to despise, were to be raised once more above them. Liam Sweeney, the Registrar for South Donegal, wrote to the Minister – 'We were directed to do all in our power to upset the working of the British Courts and now when we have done so, when British Courts are a dead letter, they are resurrected and we are ordered quietly to give way to them'. It was not even to be as simple as that. The court system, so warmly praised in the official statement, was incapable of providing an effective service. Petty Sessions were gone for good; the County Courts sat only to adjourn the applications made for malicious damages. They had no criminal jurisdiction, nor juries, and the Assizes could not go out because the country was once more 'in a disturbed state'. It is little wonder that Michael Collins, the Chairman of the Provisional Government, which had driven itself into this impasse, asked plaintively: 'What will be the procedure for bringing men to trial before a Civil Court and what Civil Courts are there to bring them before?'

There was not to be an immediate answer to the question. The recision of the 1920 Decree had left in place, temporarily, the District and Parish Courts outside Dublin City, but, without superior courts into which to feed, no decisions could be appealed nor accused sent forward for trial. Only in Dublin was there a proper hierarchy of courts in existence. The Resident Magistrates – hated almost by rote – were pensioned off to universal jubilation and late in October, twenty-seven legal gentlemen were appointed, as an emergency measure, to replace them, except that they were wisely called District Justices. Their appointment was the one good deed in a time which had seen the executive treat the judiciary as its creature. They were dispersed to various parts of the country and with patience, tact and hard work, they managed to make the transition from one system to another as seamless as possible. They may have been even helped by the fact that there were no rules on practice and procedure, and had only their knowledge of the law and their common-sense to rely upon. Neither had any thought been given to the bulk of litigation outstanding in the Dáil Courts nor the judgements that remained unexecuted. No guidance had been given to the thousands of plaintiffs and defendants left stranded by the sudden change of direction. It seems that Government Ministers had very little knowledge of the extent of the work which had been handled by the courts. Solicitors and their clients were greatly incensed by the stalemate in legal affairs where nothing could be processed and only vague promises of relief were extracted from the Ministry of Home Affairs. A full year passed before Judicial Commissioners were appointed to wind up the Dáil Courts. The effect was to revive the jurisdiction by hearing appeals and registering judgements in permanent form. It proved a lengthy and expensive reappraisal.

The debate on the Bill to wind up the courts was introduced on 19 July 1923 after a year of half-hearted efforts to bring some relief to those whose affairs were caught up in the general stagnation. The debate which followed was lively and often acrimonious. It afforded George Gavan Duffy, who had been a signatory to the Treaty, the opportunity to pay tribute to the Dáil Courts and lament their sudden closure. There was another signatory in the Chamber: Eamonn Duggan had served as Minister for Home Affairs during the critical period but his only contribution was to move the amendments on behalf of his successor, Kevin O'Higgins. For some reason, the latter chose to attack the courts, calling them channels of corruption and abuse. He grudgingly allowed that in their earlier manifestations they had provided a rough and ready settlement for minor disputes but later they existed to obstruct justice by using injunctions to prevent the public going to the established courts. It was a remarkable piece of instant historical revision. The point of the Dáil Courts was to be a compelling alternative to the statutory administration – the policy reiterated time and again by Dáil Éireann and, presumably, supported by O'Higgins. On a personal level, his speech undermined the work of decent men and women who had risked their liberty, and sometimes more, to fulfil the dream of a self-sufficient Ireland. The professional judges, two of whom were to serve as Judicial Commissioners under the Act, could hardly have welcomed the calumny being heaped upon their fitness for office, although, forty years on, the saintly Davitt would only say that the remarks were 'ungracious'. The Minister was being egregiously unreasonable, possibly because arguments with Gavan Duffy tended to unsettle him. If these courts lacked the legal decencies, reached above their station and were corrupt, by practice, then the Minister should have been asked why he was presenting a Bill to the House whose primary purpose was to give permanency to their judgements. The first section defined a Dáil Court as 'being any court which was constituted under a Decree made in the year 1920 by the Minister for Home Affairs purporting to act under the authority of Dáil Éireann constituted to be the Government of Saorstát Éireann by the members who were elected for constituencies in Ireland and who first assembled in a Parliament held in the Mansion House at Dublin on the 21st day of January 1919'.

The courts which were established by Dáil Éireann, centred on a solid base first put in place by individual communities, were part of the impetus towards a liberal democracy, evident since the beginning of the century. The proper balance of the executive, legislative and judicial roles was a concept instinctively grasped – hence the instant protest when IRA officers attempted to bully local courts, and the widespread indignation at the government *schluss* of July 1922. Judges elected by and from the people ensured that a proper element of mediation was carried over after the transition to mandatory courts. Patriotism, fear and particular hopes of a more favourable verdict were undeniable factors, but do not totally explain why the public deserted the established legal administration. Quite simply, the people supported the Dáil Courts because they suited their needs. Parties who lost their case wrote long complaints about individual justices, clerks and witnesses but only the unionist editor of the *Western News* dismissed the courts as 'an amusing cuss'. In 1925, thousands of registered judgements passed into the jurisdiction of the High Court to become part of the *res judicata*, that is, matters already decided. Today, one would be as free to produce a Dáil Court judgement to confirm a right-of-way, provided it had not been overturned, as a court order obtained last year. Not only that, but the District and Circuit Courts were directly adopted from the Dáil system. Moreover, the Dáil and the Seanad held up the passage of the Bill establishing the present Courts of Justice by eight months, to ensure that the Irish Free State Government would retain no vestige of control over its judges. Perhaps the Deputies and the Senators had learned a salutary lesson from the fate which had so swiftly overtaken the courts of Dáil Éireann.

Notes

1. Most of the information gleaned from contemporary newspapers, including the *Limerick Leader*, *Tipperary People* and the *Clonmel Chronicle*.
2. See *Retreat from Revolution: The Dáil Courts, 1920-24*, Dublin 1994, Mary Kotsonouris.
3. The Home Affairs Ministry's files and some court registers are with the records of the Dáil Courts Commission in the National Archives.

8

The Army and the Dáil-Civil/Military Relations within the Independence Movement

Eunan O'Halpin

Dr Eunan O'Halpin is Associate Professor of Government and Associate Dean for Research in Dublin City University Business School. He is the author of *The Decline of the Union: British government in Ireland, 1892-1920* (1987) and of *Head of the Civil Service: a study of Sir Warren Fisher* (1989). He is currently preparing books on Irish security policy since independence, and on Anglo-American security co-operation between 1914 and 1949.

◆◆◆◆◆◆◆◆◆◆

This paper discusses aspects of civil/military relations within the independence movement in the years immediately before and after the first meeting of Dáil Éireann on 21 January 1919. Coincidentally but symbolically, this was on the same day that two policemen were shot dead at Soloheadbeg in the first serious act of violence in the War of Independence. That day thus marked the somewhat uneasy and temporary fusion of two distinct strands in Irish nationalism, the constitutional and the revolutionary, in a unitary independence movement.

The aims of the paper are firstly to explore key issues surrounding the formation and control of the national army, and secondly to comment on the consequences for the military and for defence policy in independent Ireland of what happened in the first chaotic and violent years of Dáil Éireann's existence. The defence forces have suffered ever since from the circumstances of their establishment. Generations of Irish politicians have heaped praise on the army as the epitome of national discipline and the guarantor of national sovereignty. Successive governments have, nevertheless, failed to develop even the outlines of a credible national defence policy, while the army has been hampered in discharging its incoherent mandate by a chronic lack of money, and by a byzantine system of administration designed primarily to keep the warriors in perpetual thrall to the Department of Defence. *The Gleeson Report* of 1990 on pay and conditions in the defence forces, undoubtedly the most authoritative examination of the role and condition of the army yet published, commented that 'the Defence Forces have traditionally enjoyed high esteem and trust but their internal affairs have tended to attract a relatively low level of public and political interest. It has been observed before that armies in democracies tend, by turn, to be ignored or, at best, taken for granted and then trustingly looked to on the occasion of a variety of military emergencies. The Defence Forces in this country are no exception.'[1]

In many respects, however, the experience of the Irish defence forces *has* been exceptional when compared with those of other newly independent states. This is demonstrated by the remarkably low level of defence spending since independence, by government's deeply ingrained unwillingness to comment on defence policy except in the most anodyne terms, and by the absence of any informed debate on defence issues.

The Paradox of Irish Defence Policy

The declared primary role of the defence forces since the end of the civil war in 1923 has been to defend the state from external attack. In reality, however, successive governments have relied not on the army but on the defensive umbrella provided by Britain and her allies to shield the state from external aggression. In practice it has been the army's dismal fate since the early 1920s to subsist at a size and at a level of equipment just sufficient to perpetuate the domestic illusion that the state is committed to and capable of effective action against external aggression, and to deal with any likely internal security threat. The latter function has sometimes seen the army required to act not so much in aid of the civil power, the conventional phrase used to describe its security and other activities within the state, but in lieu of it: a striking example is the use of military courts during the civil war, in the 1930s, and again during the Emergency to administer justice for anti-state offences. The army has also had a wide miscellany of non-military jobs routinely thrust upon it. Some of these, such as helicopter search and rescue duties, derive from its military functions. Others, however, such as collecting rubbish during a bin strike, or running an emergency shelter for Dublin's homeless, are given to it simply because it is a convenient source of disciplined and obedient labour.[2]

Independent Ireland's defence policy and practice appears all the more curious given the means by which independence was won and the practical legitimacy of the new state established. The struggle against the military and police machines of the British government in Ireland was followed by a civil war in which the national army defeated armed republican resistance to the new order.[3] In such circumstances one might expect to find the military revered and cossetted by deferential ministers anxious to keep them quiet. This was scarcely the army's experience. Similarly, nationalist Ireland's enduring grievance about partition might have been expected to influence the development and organisation of the defence forces. In fact, once the border was confirmed in December 1925, the army was required to operate as though neither the political entity nor the land mass of Northern Ireland existed. This injunction left the defence forces desperately ill-informed when the Second World War broke out. It caused further difficulties when the Northern troubles flared up again in 1969 and the possibility of Irish military intervention was canvassed by ministers unfamiliar with modern military realities.[4] Finally, from 1923 the defence forces were required to plan for their nominal primary task of resisting external aggression without any consultation with or explicit reference to Britain, which until 1938 retained the treaty ports and concomitant rights to demand additional facilities in times of crisis, which controlled the seas and skies around Ireland, and which was not only the implicit strategic guarantor of Irish security but also much the most plausible threat to it.

The vicissitudes endured by the army since the early 1920s are explained partly by three historical factors. The first is the declared policy of military neutrality adopted from the outset by the Irish Free State, which over the years has acquired the status of holy writ.[5] It is outside the ambit of this paper. The second factor is the nature of the War of Independence, and the third is the ambiguous and tangled relationship between and within the military and the political wings of the independence movement after 1913.

Between 1919 and 1921 Ireland experienced a sporadic, scattered, small scale guerrilla war. Its object was not to inflict direct military defeat on a vastly superior enemy but to make the country ungovernable and to force Britain to recognise the legitimacy of Irish demands for self-rule. Ulster apart, these tactics succeeded. Their very success, however, seems to have left both a generation of political leaders, and the public at large, under the illusion that all that would ever be needed to deter or to expel an external aggressor was a few rifles in the right hands, some improvised road blocks and a landmine or two. Compulsory national service, one of the hallmarks of nervous neutrals in times of crisis, was eschewed even during World War Two. Maritime and air defence has formed no serious part of national defence policy at any time: despite British promptings from as early as 1923, until 1939 the new state chose not to attempt even to monitor shipping movements in its territorial waters, let alone to police the coastline. Even a competent fisheries protection service was beyond the ambitions of the state until Ireland joined the European Community: it was pressure and money from Brussels, not from Parkgate Street, that finally provided the naval service and the air corps with the vessels, the aircraft and the equipment to monitor Ireland's sector of Community waters. Despite the sometimes passionate urgings of the first generation of professional officers, air defence in practice has remained an almost entirely closed book.[6] With the exception of Richard Mulcahy and, arguably, Sean MacEntee, no senior politician on either side of the treaty divide after 1923 wasted their energies on the serious consideration of external defence issues until forced to do so by outside events in 1938-9. Once brought to heel in 1924, the army was used primarily as a focus for national loyalty, and as an invaluable instrument of sometimes draconian internal security policy: the IRA men executed during the Emergency were sentenced by military, not by civilian courts. Despite the chastening national defence experience of the Emergency, and the forthright warnings of the chief of staff, General McKenna, in 1945, on the need to achieve and to maintain 'a proper state of preparedness for defence' in the future, the old assumptions about the nature of external defence reasserted themselves once World War Two ended. What Tom Garvin has described as the 'extraordinary political longevity' of the revolutionary elite ensured that these views held currency at least until the early 1960s. Some would say that they persist today.[7]

Civil/Military Relations within the Independence Movement

To understand the recurrent problems of civil/military relations within the separatist movement, it is necessary to look back further than the army mutiny, the civil war, the war of independence, the creation of Dáil Éireann or even the 1916 Rising.

The contemporary defence forces are generally regarded as the direct descendants of the Irish Volunteers, formed in November 1913 as an open nationalist militia pledged to ensure that the Irish Home Rule Bill would be applied in full.[8] In June 1914 the organisation was forced to accept the control of John Redmond, who appeared on the verge of achieving a substantial measure of independence by constitutional political means as long as the British government would keep its nerve on Home Rule and face down the threat of violence from Unionist Ulster. By imposing his control on the Irish Volunteers he hoped to rein in the wilder separatist elements within the organisation whom he feared might otherwise seek confrontation with the British authorities. After the outbreak of World War One most Volunteers took their lead from Redmond, still the unchallenged leader of nationalist Ireland, and supported the British war effort. A minority of perhaps five per cent seceded, taking with them the title of the 'Irish Volunteers'. This was a significant moment because it illustrated the conditional nature of the subordination of armed to constitutional politics within the nationalist movement. Two years later came the Easter Rising, the brainchild of the Military Council of the long established secret society the IRB. It was organised behind the back of the Volunteers' chief of staff, Eoin MacNeill, by a group of his officers who ensured that the rebellion went ahead despite his countermanding order. This illustrated the conditional nature of subordination and allegiance even within the revolutionary movement, and it probably contributed to the mistrust of the IRB later displayed by some key political figures, including Eamon de Valera.[9] In launching the rebellion, the IRB proclaimed an Irish Republic, declared itself the rightful government of Ireland, and created an Irish Republican Army into which the Irish Volunteers and other nationalist combatants were automatically subsumed. From this it follows that the IRA, or the Volunteers as the organisation continued generally to be known, was the military arm of the IRB's Irish republic. The IRB itself continued as an oath bound secret society, espousing republican principles but run on strictly hierarchical lines and demanding absolute obedience from its members. It remained distinct from the IRA and from Sinn Féin, although most IRA commanders, and many of the leading figures in Sinn Féin, were also IRB members. Florence O'Donoghue, a senior figure in both the IRB and the IRA, was later to observe that this 'interlocking of leadership personnel', while it 'tended to unify policy and correlate activities' between the different separatist organisations, had serious disadvantages which later became apparent. It presented people with a bewildering and potentially conflicting set of allegiances, oaths and obligations, and it perpetuated a tradition of conspiracy within the independence movement.[10] It is in this context that the Dáil's relationship with the IRA must be reviewed.

The present Taoiseach, Albert Reynolds, recently observed that amongst the First Dáil's achievements had been the establishment of 'the primacy of the civil power' over the military.[11] While civilian primacy is now an unremarked cornerstone of Irish constitutional politics the evidence suggests, however, that the question of the ultimate loyalty of the military wing of the independence movement was a vexed one until the collapse of the army mutiny in 1924. Throughout the War of Independence, there were confusions of allegiance between the Dáil government and the IRB, and between the IRB and the IRA. After the treaty came civil war, won decisively by those willing to abandon the ideal of the pure republic in favour of the qualified independence of a 26 county free state within the British commonwealth. But a rift persisted even amongst the victors: in March 1924 a faction within the military, resentful of developments within the army since 1922, threatened the government with mutiny.[12] That crisis was overcome, but another more resilient group of challengers to the supremacy of elected civilian government endured in the republican movement: indeed, the present day Provisional IRA claims as an 'ethical fact' to be the 'legal representatives of the Irish people' and the embodiment of the republic established at Easter 1916. Their authority for this is a decision of the republican 'Second Dáil' in 1938, that 'ghostly conclave' as Sean O'Faolain unkindly termed it, to delegate its notional authority as the true government of the Irish Republic to the IRA army council in perpetuity.[13] Irish history since 1913 is littered with such legitimist claims, abandoned oaths and rival authorities. Throughout the campaign for self determination after 1913, even during what de Valera called the 'four years of magnificent discipline' from 1917 to 1921, relations between the political and military wings of the separatist movement were fraught with uncertainty.[14] That grew rather than lessened after the establishment of Dáil Éireann, although this did not become public knowledge until after the treaty was signed.

Sinn Féin's success in the 1918 election was seen as a resounding endorsement of 'the right to self-determination', to use the present Taoiseach's words once more. However, when Dáil Éireann was established it did not automatically become the sole focus of allegiance and font of legitimacy for members of the independence movement. The IRA had its own executive, dominated by but distinct from the IRB. The IRB regarded itself as the embodiment of the republic proclaimed in 1916, and saw the IRA as its army. This, together with its revolutionary and conspiratorial tradition, posed difficulties for those who sought to build on the political authority conferred by Sinn Féin's electoral success. But Sinn Féin itself appeared less a political party than the civilian and subordinate wing of the independence movement, and there were many members both of the IRA and the IRB in it. This tangle of affiliation and allegiance precluded the development of a clearcut delineation of control and responsibility between the political and the military wings of the independence movement. Indeed, the most striking aspect of relations between proto-parliament, proto-government and proto-army is not that many in the IRA came to regard the Dáil as at best an irrelevance in the independence struggle, but that the principle of civilian control of the army somehow got onto and remained on the agenda at all.

From April 1919 the Dáil government was headed by de Valera, with Cathal Brugha as Minister for Defence. The chief of staff, Richard Mulcahy, also a TD, reported to him. The evidence suggests that the two were on quite good terms, and that both sought to place the IRA unequivocally under the control of the Dáil as the legitimate parliament of the Irish people. In reality, however, neither Minister for Defence nor chief of staff had much say in what happened on the ground up to 1921. Local initiatives, such as the Soloheadbeg shootings, and the killing of a resident magistrate in Westport in March 1919, caused widespread revulsion and ran contrary to what IRA GHQ – or at any rate the chief of staff, Mulcahy – wanted. They also went against Sinn Féin's political strategy, but the Dáil government could not disown such acts without abandoning its claim to speak for the whole independence movement and losing whatever influence it had on the IRA.[15] Given these complexities, it is not surprising that the question of the ultimate control of and responsibility for the IRA was left hanging. At Brugha's behest, from the autumn of 1919 all members of the IRA were ordered to swear an oath of allegiance to the Dáil, but the army's ultimate loyalties remained unclear. Despite its claim to governance, Dáil Éireann only assumed formal responsibility for the IRA's military actions on 30 March 1921, more than two years after the war began and when earlier embarrassments such as Soloheadbeg had been balanced by a prodigious range of British atrocities. IRA volunteers could, therefore, be forgiven for maintaining allegiance to other sources of legitimacy during the campaign. The 'vast majority' of senior

IRA officers remained 'active members of the IRB', though not all regarded it as the ultimate repository of republican legitimacy - the only IRB member with whom this writer ever discussed the point, admittedly an anti-treaty man, said that all it meant to him was a levy of a few pence a week, while research suggests that the IRB's Supreme Council was virtually moribund between 1919 and December 1921.[16]

Cathal Brugha's view that ultimate authority over the IRA should lie unequivocally with Dáil Éireann was not shared by his most formidable government colleague, the Minister for Finance, Michael Collins, whose role in the conduct of the War of Independence was destined to become the subject of bitter controversy. As finance minister, Collins had no formal link with the IRA at all, while as IRA director of intelligence he was a subordinate of the chief of staff, Mulcahy. In practice his powerful personality, his control over the finances of the independence movement, his influence within Sinn Féin, his efficiency and ruthlessness as director of intelligence, and his connections through the IRB with senior IRA officers, won him unrivalled standing with the fighting men. The IRB relinquished its claim to be the legitimate government in September 1919, but under its constitution, its president remained also president *ex officio* of the Irish Republic. Its continued autonomy caused great unease to Brugha and some of his colleagues. Collins, by contrast, regarded the IRB as the nervous system of the independence movement, and used it to develop and to maintain links with local IRA leaders which paralleled, if they did not subvert, the formal chain of command between units and GHQ. During the treaty debates, Brugha denounced as 'fairy tales' the claim that Collins 'had won the war', and accused him of courting 'notoriety' during it. However, he offered no evidence to support this belittling of Collins' military role. The attack was widely regarded as a personal one rather than as a measured contribution to the anti-treaty case: the republican, Todd Andrews, who heard it, said it caused embarrassment on all sides. Some, however, have argued forcefully that Brugha's words have been misinterpreted, and that his speech should be seen as part of his efforts to challenge Collins' anti-democratic IRB machinations. One writer, bent on rescuing the memory of the struggle for the republic from the slights and distortions of foppish revisionists, has also claimed that Brugha's practical work has been systematically downplayed and Collins' unfairly exaggerated. Against this, a recent study of Mulcahy indicates that Brugha had little direct impact on the conduct of the war, while Brugha himself gave great credit to Mulcahy and the entire staff at IRA GHQ. The Brugha/Collins divide remains a sensitive one: the Taoiseach sought to bridge it by stating that the activities of 'the Volunteers on the ground' were directed 'by Michael Collins and by Cathal Brugha as minister for defence', though in so doing he completely discounted Mulcahy's work as chief of staff from 1918 to 1921 and as the maker of the national army. Whatever the respective contributions of Brugha, of Mulcahy and of IRA GHQ, it is unarguable that Collins was the man most closely identified with the military campaign by those who fought in it.[17]

During the War of Independence these problems of allegiance and control loomed large only within the separatist leadership: most IRA men were oblivious to the subtleties of overlapping and competing loyalties, since all the claimants on their fealty shared the common aim of pushing Britain out of Ireland. For practical purposes they were loyal firstly to their officers, and secondly to the Irish republic as embodied in Dáil Éireann, its president and government. As Liam Lynch wrote in 1917, when the Volunteers were reorganising in the wake of the Rising, 'We have declared for an Irish Republic and will not live under any other law' – a statement resonantly paraphrased in the title of his biography *No Other Law*. In reality, as the Anglo-Irish war progressed some recognised that that aim would require both definition and modification in due course: shortly before his death on Bloody Sunday in November 1920, Dick McKee, commandant of the Dublin Brigade, was asked by a close comrade what did he think they would get out of all our efforts. His reply was: 'Well if we clatter [sic] them hard enough we might get Dominion Home Rule'.[18]

Most IRA men lacked McKee's prescience, and were dismayed by the terms of the treaty: it seemed a grubby compromise which forsook all the symbolic elements of independence central to republican thought. Todd Andrews wrote that 'for years I had lived on a plane of emotional idealism, believing that we were being led by great men into a new Ireland'. He recalled the utter shock of most of the fighting men during the treaty debates both at the willingness of so many TDs, above all Collins, to compromise on independence, and at the bitterness which emerged. The Dáil's acceptance of the treaty was followed by a succession of splits within the independence movement. The majority of officers at GHQ, the majority of the Supreme Council of the IRB, the majority of the government of Dáil Éireann, the majority of TDs, and above all the clear majority of voters in the May 1922 election, came out in favour of the treaty. Within the IRA things were different: desperate efforts to preserve unity made by Collins, now president of the IRB, Mulcahy, and anti-treaty IRA commanders, foundered. In rejecting the treaty, the IRA pushed the IRB aside, and more importantly abjured its oath of allegiance to Dáil Éireann. Thereafter, it would sometimes regard itself as the senior partner, but never the servant, of any civilian authority: in October 1922, in a curious inversion of conventional democratic theory, the IRA executive established a 'Republican Government' effectively subordinate to it.[19] By a sad irony Cathal Brugha, once the champion of the theory of elected civilian control of the armed forces, met a brave death fighting against it; Michael Collins, whose conspiratorial approach to politics begged questions about the strength of his own democratic convictions, died the practical defender of the popularly elected Dáil Éireann's right to decide the nation's destiny.

Conclusion

There is no doubt that independent Ireland's peculiar approach to national defence has its origins in developments between 1913 and 1924, and the attendant complications of multiple and divided allegiances amongst the separatist elite. The bruising experience of civil/military relations during the independence struggle left the first generation of politicians on both sides of the treaty divide with a profound and understandable fear of the intermingling of politics and military affairs, and of the operation of competing systems of allegiance within the army. In November 1924 the Cosgrave government finally disposed of the problem by banning military membership of oathbound or secret societies. Once it had been purged of politics and of insubordination, the army was reduced virtually to nothing: in 1936 a staff officer wrote that the country 'may be said to be not relatively but absolutely disarmed', and that the public 'do not realise that in the usual European sense the Saorstát can hardly be said to have a Defence Force at all'[20]. That was the result of a policy of calculated neglect of military affairs, adopted when the Cosgrave administration decided that the surest way to keep civilian government strong was to keep the army weak, whatever the consequences for national defence. It is a precept which all subsequent governments have wholeheartedly endorsed.

Notes

1. *Report of the Commission on Remuneration and Conditions of Service in the Defence Forces* [the Gleeson report] (Stationery Office, Dublin, 1990), p. 13.
2. *Gleeson report*, pp. 17-18. In December 1992 the Taoiseach announced that the army would provide and staff a temporary shelter for the homeless people in Dublin over the Christmas period. In the event, the army remained saddled with this task for a full year.
3. The best account of the Anglo-Irish struggle is Charles Townshend, *The British Campaign in Ireland, 1919-1921: The Development of Political and Military Policies* (Oxford University Press, Oxford, 1975). The most authoritative analysis of the civil war is Michael Hopkinson, *Green against green: the Irish civil war, 1922-23* (Gill & Macmillan, Dublin, 1988).
4. See Eunan O'Halpin, 'Army, politics and society, 1923-1945', in TG Fraser and Keith Jeffery (eds.), *Men, women and war: Historical Studies XVIII* (Lilliput, Dublin, 1993), pp. 163-7; interview with the late Colonel Dan Bryan, July 1983; information from a retired staff officer, June 1992.
5. On this vexed subject see Patrick Keatinge, *A singular stance: Irish neutrality in the 1980s* (Institute of Public Administration, Dublin, 1984) and Trevor Salmon, *Unneutral Ireland: an ambivalent and unique security policy* (Clarendon Press, Oxford, 1989).
6. *Gleeson report*, p. 280; information from a serving officer, 1994; AA Quigley, *Green is my sky* (Avoca Publications, Dublin, 1983), pp.123-4.
7. Tom Garvin, *Nationalist revolutionaries in Ireland, 1858-1928* (Clarendon Press, Oxford, 1987), p. 141.
8. JP Duggan, *A History of the Irish Army* (Gill and Macmillan, Dublin, 1991,) p.1.
9. Eunan O'Halpin, *The Decline of the Union: British Government in Ireland, 1892-1920* (Gill and Macmillian, Dublin 1987), pp. 112-15.
10. John O'Beirne-Ranelagh, *The IRB from the Treaty to 1924*, Irish Historical Studies vol. xx, no. 77 (March 1977), pp. 26-27; Florence O'Donoghue, *No Other Law* (The Irish Press, Dublin 1954), p.17.
11. Speech by the Taoiseach, Mansion House, Dublin, 26 Apr. 1994.
12. Maryann Gialanella Valiulis, *Portrait of a Revolutionary: General Richard Mulcahy and the Founding of the Irish Free State* (Irish Academic Press, Dublin, 1992), pp. 199-235.
13. Sean O'Faolain, *De Valera* (Penguin, London, 1939), p. 114. The most recent exposition of the republican argument that the republican second Dáil was the sole repository of legitimacy following de Valera's apostasy

in 1925/6 can be found in Brian P. Murphy, *Patrick Pearse and the Lost Republican Ideal* (James Duffy, Dublin, 1991).

14. *Official Report: Debate on the Treaty between Great Britain and Ireland signed in London on the 6th December 1921* [the Treaty debates] (Stationery Office, Dublin, n.d.), p. 347, 7 Jan. 1992.

15. Valiulis, *Richard Mulcahy*, p. 39. Dan Breen, *My Fight for Irish freedom* (The Talbot Press, Dublin, 1924; Anvil Press, Tralee, 1964), pp. 41-2; Desmond Ryan, *Sean Tracey and the Third Tipperary Brigade IRA* (The Kerryman, Tralee, 1945; Anvil Press, Tralee, n.d.), p. 59, says that even militant Volunteers believed that the Soloheadbeg ambush had been a 'bungled business'. See pp. 57-66 for a detailed discussion of the ambush intended to dispose of the widely aired charge that the killings were unjustified and unworthy.

16. O'Beirne-Ranelagh, 'The IRB from the Treaty to 1924', p. 31; conversation with my late grandfather Jim Moloney, who served on Liam Lynch's staff as director of communications in 1922/3, 1978. He was a brother of Con Moloney, adjutant general and later deputy chief of staff of the republican forces. Their father PJ Moloney was a member of the first and second Dáils.

17. O' Beirne-Ranelagh, 'The IRB from the Treaty to 1924', p. 31; *Treaty Debates*, pp. 326-7, 7 Jan. 1922; CS Andrews, *Dublin Made Me: an autobiography* (The Mercier Press, Dublin 1979), p. 207; on the respective contributions of Brugha and Mulcahy see Valiulis, *Richard Mulcahy*, pp. 41-77; for a recent though traditionalist republican analysis of Collins' role, see Murphy, *Patrick Pearse and the Lost Republican Ideal*; speech by An Taoiseach, as in note 11 above.

18. Andrews, *Dublin Made Me*, pp. 201-7; O'Donoghue, *No Other Law*, p. 18; conversations with Todd Andrews and with Jim Moloney, 1982 and 1978 respectively; General Liam Archer to Professor Michael Hayes, 26 June 1969, University College Dublin Archives, Hayes papers, p. 53/344. Archer, a Collins man, took the pro-treaty side. He became a regular soldier, serving as o/c signals, as director of intelligence, and ultimately as chief of staff of the defence forces.

19. Andrews, *Dublin made me*, p. 207; O'Donoghue, *No other law*, pp. 276-7 and 342-3. The republican government was established through an army executive resolution proposed by Con Moloney.

20. 'Fundamental factors affecting Irish defence policy', a document marked 'G2/0057, dated May 1936', with private secretary, Minister for Defence, to private secretary, Minister for Finance, 23 May 1936, UCD, MacEntee papers, p67/191. The principal author of this paper was the late Colonel Dan Bryan, then deputy director of intelligence.

9

Local Government and the First Dáil

Mary A Daly

Mary A Daly is Associate Professor of Modern Irish History at University College Dublin. Educated at University College Dublin and Oxford University, she is a member of the Royal Irish Academy. Her publications include *Dublin: the Deposed Capital, 1890-1914* (Cork 1984) and *Industrial Development and Irish National Identity, 1922-39* (Dublin 1922). She is currently completing a history of the Department of the Environment.

◆◆◆◆◆◆◆◆◆◆

The story of the First Dáil is generally viewed as a Dublin-based event with deputies and ministers braving the risk of arrest to attend its sessions and conduct Dáil business. Republican activity outside Dublin during the years 1919-21 is assumed to have been a purely military experience with small numbers of young men and women engaged in arms raids, attacks on RIC stations or guerrilla warfare. Ordinary people feature only as occasional victims, or as providers of food and shelter. An account of local government during the years of the First Dáil inevitably focuses on provincial Ireland, on the local politics rather than on military activity and on the actions of ordinary men and women. From the summer of 1920 numerous local councillors, officials, rate collectors and even rate payers participated in the establishment of an alternative administration. The Dáil Éireann Ministry of Local Government functioned as a real government department, not only attempting to keep the local government system in operation despite civil unrest, but also embarking on fundamental reforms which were continued by the Government of the Irish Free State.

The pre-1918 Sinn Féin movement had a strong tradition in local government. By 1911 Sinn Féin controlled twelve of the eighty seats on Dublin Corporation and ten per cent of those elected to Dáil Éireann had previous experience in local government. On Dublin Corporation, where Sinn Féin provided the major opposition to the dominant nationalist membership, it attacked the jobbery, corruption and inefficiency of the existing administration. Arthur Griffith's editorials in the newspaper *Sinn Féin* regularly excoriated both corrupt local authorities and the inefficiency of the Local Government Board.[1] Yet despite the party's long association with local government, the subject appears to have been given a low priority by Dáil Éireann. WT Cosgrave, a long-standing member of Dublin Corporation, was given charge of Local Government in April 1919 and a committee of ten TDs was appointed to assist him in preparing a Local Government policy. The deputies' interest centred on housing and reform of the Poor Law, which were then the most pressing concerns at grass-roots level.[2] The 1919 Housing (Ireland) Act had recently introduced a generous package of grants and subsidised loans to encourage the construction of houses for the working class. Many Irish local authorities were keen to take advantage of the Act in the hope of ridding Irish towns and cities of their slums. There was also a long-standing ambition among many shades of nationalist opinion to dismantle the Poor Law system on the grounds that workhouses were both unpopular and expensive. In 1919, however, the Dáil was in no position to tackle Poor Law reform and, as there was no money available to provide loans or subsidies for housing, the committee of TDs recommended that Irish councils should proceed 'full steam ahead' to avail of the generous facilities provided under recent British Government housing legislation. Dáil Éireann duly issued 2,000 circulars containing this advice to Sinn Féin clubs throughout the country. What the Local Government Board – Dublin Castle's controlling body for Irish local government – thought of this unexpected publicity for their housing programme is unknown. During 1919 most Irish councils and Poor Law boards continued to deal normally with the Local Government Board, sending deputations to the Custom House, forwarding the minutes of meetings and submitting their accounts for audit by Local Government Board.[3]

The year 1920 marks the true beginnings of the Dáil Ministry of Local Government. Elections held in all urban district councils and county boroughs in January 1920 gave Sinn Féin control of 72 out of 127 councils, though often by a narrow majority; the Labour Party had also polled extremely well. The Dáil's request that councils pledge allegiance to Dáil Éireann brought a luke-warm response; urban and municipal councils were reluctant to act independently of county and rural councils which still remained outside Sinn Féin control. However, when Sinn Féin won control of 28 out of 33 county councils and 182 out of 206 rural councils following local elections held in June 1920, the majority of county councils and rural district councils, as instructed, passed resolutions of allegiance to 'the authority of Dáil Éireann as the duly elected Government of the Irish People'.[4]

What would happen next remained uncertain. WT Cosgrave had been arrested in March 1920 and Kevin O'Higgins became substitute Minister, the job in which he first established his reputation as a powerful political figure. The Local Government Committee which Cosgrave had established in the previous year had apparently collapsed; O'Higgins superseded it with a small committee of men with practical experience of local government: the lord mayors of Cork and Limerick, the accountants of Kerry County Council and Dublin city and the secretary of Monaghan County Council. The committee began to examine the financial and legal implications of local authorities breaking all links with the Local Government Board, but by the date of the local elections in June 1920 the Cabinet had not decided on a course of action. At the end of June, some weeks after the local elections, the Dáil appointed a further commission containing nineteen men and one woman, Jenny Wyse Power, including TDs, councillors and local officials, to examine the possibility of operating Irish local administration without British government loans and grants. However, on 29 July, before the commission held its first meeting, the British-controlled Local Government Board forced the issue. All local authorities were required to give formal evidence of their allegiance to the Local Government Board by undertaking to submit their accounts for audit and to obey all the Board's rules; failure to do so would result in the loss of all Local Government Board grants. This action·was apparently ordered by the British Prime Minister, Bonar Law, against the advice of the Dublin Local Government Board. Most local authorities severed all links with the Board as a result of the ultimatum. By September 1920, two months after it had been issued, only counties Antrim, Armagh and Derry had given the formal assurances sought by the Board; many councils formally burned the circular or minuted that they had placed it in the wastebasket. However, Kilkenny County Council appears to have had no formal links with the Dáil Ministry until the spring of 1921 and some rural district councils tried to maintain relations with both the Dáil and the Local Government Board.

A formal breach with the Local Government Board meant the loss of £1.6m in grants, approximately one-fifth of the income of local authorities plus the end of cheap housing loans and grants for road improvements, hard facts which explain the Dáil's reluctance to order such a break. By the summer of 1920, however, these losses were dwarfed in some parts of Ireland by the malicious injury rates levied on local councils to pay for the cost of property damaged in the course of the Anglo-Irish war by both republicans and crown forces. In County Cork the cost of malicious injuries was almost six times the value of Local

Government Board grants which the county lost. Breaking with the Local Government Board would permit local authorities to avoid levying malicious injury rates. Despite this benefit, and the Sinn Féin landslide in the local elections, local authorities often proved loath to lose access to grants for housing, roads and drainage, and many councils which had sworn allegiance to Dáil Éireann also tried to claim road grants from the British administration. The fact that these came from the Ministry of Transport appeared to offer a loophole, though this was rapidly closed. Although road grants, housing finance and the substantial annual grant to cover the cost of agricultural rates were no longer available to Sinn Féin councils, the British proved surprisingly conciliatory on some other matters. County Committees of Agriculture continued to obtain assistance from the Department of Agriculture and, most important of all, although the Local Government Board also administered Old Age Pensions, neither they nor Dáil Éireann made any effort to disrupt the process of claiming pensions: if they had done so the loyalty of many so-called republicans might not have stood the test.

Breaking with the Local Government Board left all local authorities short of money; it also threatened the legal basis of rate collection. Rate collectors were legally obliged to lodge all rates to the treasurer, a local bank which had been officially designated by the Lord Lieutenant. Failure to do so meant that the rate collector had not discharged his obligations and could be liable to forfeit the substantial sureties he had deposited on his appointment. A rate payer whose rates were not ultimately lodged to the treasurer also ran the risk of being deemed in arrears, even if the rate collector had been paid. However, money lodged to the treasurer could be impounded by the British authorities to pay malicious injuries judgements. The Dáil was uncertain how to act on this matter, as were most local authorities. Clare County Council – who was to the forefront in the local government revolution, came to the rescue. Even before the Local Government Board ultimatum had been issued in July 1920, the council had dismissed the bank as its treasurer and decided that rates would be paid into the private accounts of three trustworthy men, whose names were not publicly known. They, in turn, would transfer the money to the council permitting them to pay the wages of council workers, food and heating bills of workhouses and other essential bills.[5] The Dáil Department instructed all counties to follow this model and the majority tried to do so, though not without difficulty.

Continuing to operate the local government system after the transfer of allegiance to Dáil Éireann proved hazardous. Local authority premises were raided by Crown forces who seized rate collectors' books and other records in an effort to make the system unworkable; several council offices were burned; county council chairmen and leading councillors were often arrested, as were some rate collectors. Cosgrave was convinced that the Crown forces had deliberately targeted the most capable councillors in counties Meath and Westmeath in the hope that their absence would mean a collapse of local government. So many members of Cork County Council were on the run that meetings were few and far between; when Clifden Board of Guardians was on the point of declaring allegiance to Dáil Éireann the building where they were meeting was surrounded by Crown forces. County secretaries, accountants and surveyors, who were often elderly men unlikely to be sympathetic to Dáil Éireann, were occasionally suspected of harbouring loyalties to the British administration and could not always be trusted. Irrespective of their political opinions these senior council officials were in an invidious position: caught between the demands of popularly-elected councillors and the legal requirements of their office. They often faced writs from the Local Government Board ordering them to hand over council books for audit. Rate collectors in County Wexford resigned *en masse* when the council dismissed the bank as treasurer. Rate collection fell heavily into arrears in many counties, perhaps because the end of the post-war boom left farmers in difficult financial circumstances, or because rate payers, who were unsympathetic to Sinn Féin, were not prepared to contribute to a rebel county council. However, many defaulters were simply opportunists who took advantage of political uncertainty: one Offaly rate collector who tried to collect rates from a leading republican was publicly threatened and abused. In County Monaghan, which had a sizeable unionist population, the heaviest arrears were in the staunchly Sinn Féin area of Carrickmacross.

By December 1920 the system of rate collection appeared to be in a virtual state of collapse; unpaid bills mounted and many local authorities were facing bankruptcy. Having dismissed the banks as treasurers they were unable to obtain overdrafts. In addition some banks appear to have co-operated with the British authorities in identifying the private accounts which were being used to operate council finances, though there are other instances of sympathetic local bank managers assisting the Sinn Féin administration. A group of rate collectors passed a resolution threatening to stop work pending a settlement between the Dáil and the Local Government Board. The introduction of martial law into most of Munster and the threat that it would be further extended brought fears that it would mean a collapse of republican local government in these areas. Several councils, working in alliance, began to reinstate the bank as treasurer, contrary to orders from Dublin. In January 1921 the Dáil reluctantly approved their actions and also promised a loan of £100,000 for hard-pressed councils. This appears to have brought an improvement in finances, though rate collection problems persisted, particularly in western counties, and were to remain the most pressing issue throughout these years.

Despite the unsettled times, the Dáil Ministry was determined to preserve the integrity, solvency and efficiency of local government and to root out inefficiency or corruption, while simultaneously introducing economies which would compensate for the loss of grant assistance from the Local Government Board. Despite the fact that this was an underground administration, the close supervision, which had been carried out by the Local Government Board, was continued almost unchanged by the Dáil Ministry. Councils were required to send minutes of all meetings to the Dáil Ministry for scrutiny. Correspondence was to be addressed to private individuals at innocuous Dublin addresses from where it would be brought to the Ministry's offices in Dublin City Hall, though one or two naive or obtuse councils wrote directly to the Dáil Ministry at Dublin's Mansion House. When Listowel Urban District Council did so, Kevin O' Higgins replied that he could not decide whether to attribute their action to 'crass stupidity or malice'.

The people who turned the Dáil Ministry of Local Government into a reality were the inspectors: twenty or so men and at least three women who travelled throughout Ireland incognito, enforcing the wishes of Cosgrave, O'Higgins and the small team of Dublin-based officials. The work was difficult and dangerous; inspectors were often followed by Crown forces, one who was arrested had difficulty in obtaining back-pay for his time in prison – eventually he was awarded half-pay. They were continually on the move from town to town and were often transferred from one part of the country to the other at short notice. Danger did not lie exclusively at the hands of the Crown Forces. One inspector who tried to persuade a hostile crowd in Leitrim of the need to pay rates was forced to make his escape by firing a gun over his head. The inspectors reported back in detail to Dublin about the state of local administration and particularly about its shortcomings: drunken or incompetent clerks, senior officials who rarely attended at the office, corrupt workhouse masters suspected of pilfering the stores. One assistant surveyor in Co. Mayo found guilty of repeated insubordination to council orders and of gross irregularities in handling money and awarding employment, had authored numerous anonymous letters in the local newspaper signed FUR (Fed-Up Ratepayer). He was dismissed. Whether the behaviour reported in this and many other cases, such as the official who never appeared in the office before noon because he insisted on attending daily Mass, was typical of Irish local administration under the Local Government Board, or whether it was merely a reflection of declining standards at a time of political instability is something we shall never know. The records of the Local Government Board which would have answered this question perished in the Custom House Fire in 1921.

The Dáil Ministry worked hard to preserve a professional and impartial local administration. Many Sinn Féin councillors believed that local authority officials, who were not obvious Sinn Féin supporters, should be fired and their jobs given to prominent local republicans. Kildare County Council was not unique in passing a resolution that none but republicans were to be employed as office staff with preference being given to members of the Volunteers. They were reminded that this was a clear violation of a Dáil Decree forbidding the imposition of any religious or political tests on public servants and were forced to withdraw the resolution, on Cosgrave's orders. Unless officials were openly hostile to Dáil Éireann to the extent that they refused to co-operate, proposals that they be dismissed or suspended were firmly resisted; fewer than five senior local authority officials appear to have been suspended on political grounds. When job vacancies emerged they were filled where possible by competitive examination, despite severe pressures to the contrary. An examination, which was being held to fill the post of secretary to the new county home in Killarney in December 1921, was interrupted by three armed and masked men who seized the completed answers and the forthcoming paper in accountancy.

They left behind a notice warning that, 'It was unfair to allow shirkers and slackers to secure positions whilst men were suffering in jail'. Despite these threats the Dáil inspector set alternative papers and the examination resumed. All sides were placated when the first-place candidate withdrew in favour of the runner-up – an ex-internee. Local pressure also sought to ensure that those appointed, even to lowly positions such as store-keeper were required to display a knowledge of Irish: however, in many cases this requirement had to be waived when none of the applicants could meet the standard.

Inspectors also encouraged reluctant rate collectors to do their job more efficiently; when this proved unsuccessful they occasionally enlisted the aid of local Volunteers to help collect rates. Rate collection in Clare passed almost entirely into the hands of the Volunteers. However, there is evidence, particularly in some Western counties, of a determination to keep local government in civilian hands, and to limit the potential power of the Volunteers. Inspectors also attempted to persuade local councils to withstand pressures from local republicans or trade union leaders, who were determined to maximise the numbers employed on road works or maintained on outdoor relief at a time when most councils were virtually bankrupt and could not pay their bills. This was a serious problem. The wartime boom had ended and tillage acreage was in decline leaving many rural workers unemployed. Matters were scarcely helped by the Anglo-Irish War. Road workers protested that senior officials, such as the county surveyor or the county secretary, continued to receive full pay, though they often had little work to do, while council labourers were unemployed, and they called for 'equality of sacrifice' among all employees. Yet, although the Dáil Ministry was sympathetic to the plight of the unemployed, when caught between demands for work and the need for prudent spending, they invariably favoured economy. In response to a query about unemployed road workers in County

Laoighis, Kevin O' Higgins wrote to the Inspector, 'You can take it that the Department's attitude is that these men should be re-employed if at all possible'. However, he added, 'Men should not be re-employed if the County Council is not in a position to pay wages regularly and in future men must not be kept at work after a condition arises which makes punctual payment impossible'. In some areas local pressures overcame the strictures from Dublin with results which occasionally verged on anarchy. In County Leitrim, the Volunteers took command, hiring road workers and gangers and designating the roads to be repaired, sending the bills to the county council. One man wrote to the Leitrim County Surveyor as follows, 'I put my clame (sic) before Kiltyclogher (Sinn Féin) Club today. I am the man that is appointed there is no change in my section. You will have a letter today from the secretary of the Club. There is a part of my section vekry bad can I fell the ruts'. In most counties, however, expenditure was kept in reasonably firm check, though problems with both expenditure and rate collection proved greatest in western areas.

All councils which declared their allegiance to Dáil Éireann were instructed to introduce economies. Most councils immediately voted to dispense with sheep dipping – an economy which found little favour with Dublin. Nor did the decision of some councils to end public health inspections of dairies, or Laoighis County Council's decision to suspend the School Attendance Act find favour. Despite straitened circumstances several councils enthusiastically endorsed a proposal from Cork County Council to establish a system of film censorship; many voted generous salary increases for the chaplains attached to local hospitals or the new county homes. The above examples suggest that the Dáil Ministry and local councils did not always agree on expenditure priorities. The Dáil believed that the reform of the Poor Law offered the greatest hopes of saving money. This proved a universally popular policy, until it was actually implemented.

They visited all workhouses and district hospitals and drew up plans for reorganisation. Poor law unions were abolished and health and poor relief was restructured on a county basis. Workhouses were closed; orphans were boarded with families, widows and other able-bodied inmates were granted home assistance. Those remaining, mainly the elderly and infirm were transferred to a county home – one per county. A county hospital was provided to treat the sick. These plans meant the closure of numerous workhouses and district hospitals. Many of the institutions threatened with closure had been half empty for many years; closing them would save considerable sums of money. However, jobs would be lost and local district hospitals would disappear. Protests were rife. 'Where', asked a councillor protesting at the threatened closure of the hospital in Callan, Co. Kilkenny, 'does self-determination come in, are the people of Callan to be ignored when they call for the preservation of the Hospital'. At the height of the War of Independence local constituency interests threatened the unity of Dáil Éireann. Wexford TDs attempted to thwart the Ministry's amalgamation plans in their area. The East Mayo Brigade of the IRA opposed the proposed closure of Swinford hospital on the grounds that it was the Brigade hospital. Disputes over the location of the new county home and county hospital were equally vocal. Carrick-on-Shannon's failure to secure one of these institutions prompted a hostile resolution from the local Sinn Féin club, a letter of protest from the parish priest and a sermon condemning the whole programme of Poor Law reform from a visiting priest. Church-state conflicts reared their head as religious sisters made redundant by the closure of workhouse hospitals battled against lay nurses for control of the new county hospitals and county homes.

On the issue of Poor Law reform, as on other matters, there is clear evidence of tensions between local and central interests. The inspector organising Poor Law reform in Cork reported: 'I had to move very delicately as these people here are convinced that they have nothing to learn from Dublin and that they are quite capable of amalgamating their County without our intervention'. Such tensions were not eased by the abrasive and uncompromising attitude often shown by Kevin O'Higgins to the difficulties which local councils faced in enforcing rate collection or unpopular economies. For many Irish people local concerns with jobs, roads or hospitals loomed larger than the struggle for national independence.

The problems facing the Dáil Ministry of Local Government were not eased by the Truce in July 1921. In fact, pressure to enforce malicious injuries rates intensified and large ratepayers such as railway companies were forced to pay their rates to malicious injury claimants rather than to the councils. Demands from labour interests for higher wages and greater expenditure on roads escalated because of the common belief that grants withheld by the British Government would soon be released. Many of these difficulties persisted during 1922 and into the early years of the Irish Free State.

The Local Government Ministry of the First Dáil provided the blue-print for local government administration under Cumann na nGaedheal. The process of abolishing the Poor Law and public health and social welfare on a county basis was continued in the 'twenties. Rural district councils were abolished and their powers were also transferred to county councils, further enhancing the county as the key agency in local administration. The establishment of the Local Appointments Commission ensured that appointments were made on merit. Economy and good housekeeping remained key considerations in the early years of the new state and the establishment of the Local Appointments Commission guaranteed that posts were filled on merit. The drive for economy and solvency continued. British politicians and Irish unionists had often claimed that Irish self-government would be synonymous with corruption and inefficiency. The performance of the Dáil Ministry for Local Government during the years 1920-22 utterly belied such fears. On a more subdued note it also showed that self-government would not bring any magic transformation in the lives of Irish people who continued to be faced with unemployment, poor housing and rates demands.

Notes

1. Richard Davis, *Arthur Griffith and non–violent Sinn Féin* (Dublin 1974) pp 132–36; Mary A Daly, *Dublin: The Deposed Capital, 1860–1914.* (Cork, 1984) p. 217-8
2. Dáil Éireann, published debates of the First Dáil are one of the essential sources for this subject.
3. The Minutes books of the Local Government Board are virtually the only records which survived the Custom House Fire in May 1921.
4. Information on this, and on most of the remainder of this essay comes from the Dáil Éireann Local Government Department (DELG) files in the National Archives. Files are listed on county by county, with specific series for the county council, urban councils, rural district councils and Poor Law boards though there are inevitable gaps. (Dublin 1977).
5. For Clare see David Fitzpatrick, *Politics and Irish Life, 1913–21. Provincial Experiences of War and Revolution.* (Dublin 1977).

10

The Significance of the First Dáil

Joe Lee

Professor Joe Lee is currently Professor of History at UCC and has been an Independent Senator since 1993. Born in Tralee in 1942, he was educated at UCD and The Institute of European History, Mainz, Germany. During his distinguished academic career he has lectured abroad in the capacity of visiting professor and was President of the Irish Association for European Studies (1983-1987). His published works include *Ireland 1912-1985: Politics and Society* and *The Modernization of Irish Society, 1848-1918.* He was awarded the Irish Times Prize for Literature (non-fiction) in 1991, the Sunday Independent/Irish Life Arts Award, 1990 and the James S Donnelly Senior Prize of American Committee of Irish Studies, 1990.

◆◆◆◆◆◆◆◆◆◆

Only 27 of the representatives elected for the 105 constituencies, all Sinn Féiners, were recorded in the attendance roll as present at the ceremonial opening on 21 January 1919. Most of the remaining members for the 73 seats won by Sinn Féin were in jail. None of the 26 Unionists or 6 Home Rulers took their seats. Although Unionists and Home Rulers agreed on little else – few had denounced the 'two-nations theory' of Irish history more vehemently than John Redmond – they both rejected Sinn Féin's abstentionist policy from Westminster, and pursued their own abstentionist policies from the Dáil. It is tempting to speculate on what might have happened on that opening day if the Unionists and Home Rulers had responded to the invitation to participate. Had all 32 members turned up, resolved to resist Sinn Féin's abstentionist policy, they would have enjoyed a majority on that issue. The opening might then have been far less ceremonial. Of course, had there been any danger of that in the real world, the invitations would hardly have been issued in the first place.

The real world, however, intruded only fitfully into the initial proceedings of the First Dáil. In the absence of any opposition in a one-party assembly, the pious unanimity with which resolutions about righting Ireland's ancient wrongs were endorsed, in an atmosphere more conducive to declamation than debate, conveyed an exaggerated sense of countrywide solidarity.

Sinn Féin had indeed won a handsome election victory, though some of its enemies frantically sought to manipulate the results to deny this obvious fact. But the very scale of the victory tempted Sinn Féin to assume that nobody else mattered at all.

Sinn Féin inherited a situation from the Home Rule Party where Ulster was top of the agenda in Anglo-Irish relations. With the Republic now elevated to that position, Ulster was relegated to second position. The Dáil chose to behave as if Ulster could thereby be simply wished away. It could not. It may well be that nothing could have come of any Dáil attempt to pursue a more constructive line. The odds were stacked against it. But the Dáil did not seriously contemplate any alternative approach.

The Dáil began with the Ulster question as dogmatically as its successors would long continue, when Cathal Brugha declared, as Ceann Comhairle, that if the absentees weren't prepared to join in the struggle to drive out the English, the deed would be done without them. This was a valid response to the absent Home Rulers. But who would drive the English from the areas represented by the absent Unionist members from Ulster? Only three Sinn Féin deputies represented constituencies within what would become Northern Ireland. In practical terms, the First Dáil was already a partition Parliament before the Better Government of Ireland Act of 1920 imposed the present line of partition.

The Dáil proved utterly ineffectual in responding to that Act, which proceeded to establish a separate jurisdiction of Northern

Ireland without reference to the Dáil, which may as well not have existed while the line of partition was imposed by British diktat.

In its treatment of the Ulster issue, the First Dáil failed to rise above the level of statesmanship displayed in the Belfast Boycott, which it endorsed in the autumn of 1920. Whatever case could be made for this, much of the Dáil discussion might as well have been about a foreign country, so little understanding did many deputies display of either political or power realities. Ernest Blythe, a Northern Protestant, one of the few members to know something of what he was talking about, made the first of numerous courageous but futile attempts to educate nationalists into Northern realities. There were a few other attempts to contemplate Unionists as potential countrymen rather than as enemies to be coerced. While Michael Collins insisted that 'there was no Ulster question', and supported the proposed boycott, he 'protested, however, against the attempt which had been made by two Deputies from the North of Ireland to inflame the passions of members'.

A glimmer of a realisation that there was an 'Ulster question', however 'Ulster' might be defined, can be detected in A MacCabe's proposal to establish a Commission to, *inter alia*:

Consider the East Ulster Question with special reference to the demand of the corner counties for local self-government, enquire into the feasibility or advisability of putting before the country a scheme of federalised Government with the county as the Unit, and ascertain how far the objections of the people of Belfast and the corner counties to an Irish Republic may be met by a liberal scheme of devolution based on this idea.[1]

Nothing came of this. The First Dáil's attitude to Ulster Unionism was as uncertain and opportunistic as that of Home Rulers earlier, and of Dublin governments for long afterwards. Not only was it opportunistic. It was also futile. The circumstances were of course far from conducive to coherent reflection, and if the

Dáil did not do better, neither did it do worse than Parnell or Redmond, although these operated under much less immediate pressure. It can be argued that the Dáil's righteousness and opportunism pale into insignificance compared with the insouciance of British and Ulster Unionist righteousness and opportunism on the line of the border. But it can also be argued that the onus was on the Dáil to display the higher statesmanship, and that in this it failed.

Apart from Cathal Brugha's brusque dismissal, the Dáil took no cognisance of the voluntary absentees. The first two documents promulgated, the Declaration of Independence and the Message to the Free Nations of the World, inevitably embodied standard nationalist rhetoric. That was the platform on which Sinn Féin had stood, and was the basis of their democratic mandate. Ironically, the third document, the Democratic Programme, had no democratic mandate. The original Programme, largely formulated by Tom Johnson of Labour, apparently as a compensatory crumb to the Labour Party for having withdrawn from the 1918 election, and to enhance the international profile of an independent Irish Labour movement, envisaged a highly interventionist role for the state. Even when diluted by more representative Sinn Féin members, it was still arguably more statist than the electorate, which consisted predominantly of men and women of small and medium property, not of no property, would have endorsed.

The appointment of a Minister for Labour by de Valera must also be regarded as something of a sop to Labour. The Department did arbitrate in a number of disputes, but it is now remembered mainly because de Valera appointed Countess Markiewicz as Minister. However genuine her solicitude for the weak and the poor, it was more on her nationalist record, as a veteran of the 1916 Rising, 'the bravest woman ever born in any country', in Cathal Brugha's ringing words, than for her social conscience, that she was appointed. The Department did not survive the early Free

State, and would not be resurrected until Seán Lemass established a Department of Labour, in very different circumstances, nearly fifty years later.

While the adoption of the Democratic Programme and the appointment of a Minister for Labour can be seen as standard moves in the political game, it may be that the First Dáil had more potential for social reform policy than could be achieved in the circumstances. In proposing the Message to the Irish Abroad, on 10 April, Eoin MacNeill, not noted for social radicalism, observed that:

... a programme of social reform and reconstruction that not long ago might be looked upon as revolutionary, but must now be regarded as practical and moderate, has been recently issued on behalf of the American Bishops and is destined to have enormous influence in evolving a new social order. Amongst the declaration included in that manifesto were the following: 'That no woman should retain any occupation which was harmful to her health or morals; that if employed they should receive the same pay as men for equal work; that there was no reason why workers should not have more than a living wage if industry could support it; that bad housing should be abolished by the State; unjust manipulation by unnecessary middlemen should be suppressed by law; the curse of incessant profiteering should be frozen out by cooperative enterprise; that until the worker has been made self-supporting insurance against unemployment and old age should be provided by a levy on industry supplemented by the State when necessary; that there should be vocational training for the young, but not to the detriment of a measure of liberal education.'

The new Irish state would take as little cognisance of many of these sentiments as of the Democratic Programme. One might speculate that had Sinn Féin remained united, Free State social policy might have been more adventurous. But this might in turn be doubted when we look at the practice, as distinct from the rhetoric, of the First Dáil. The members were well aware that they primarily represented those with a modest, but firm, stake in the country. There was therefore no doubting their determination to suppress attempts by the landless to occupy land, having resisted as early as 4 April 1919 the more radical proposal by A MacCabe and Countess Markiewicz 'that this Assembly pledges itself to a fair and full redistribution of the vacant land and ranches of Ireland among the uneconomic holders and landless men'.

If the Dáil's social instincts were broadly conservative, it may be that its economic impulses were somewhat more adventurous. The developmental philosophy of Arthur Griffith's original Sinn Féin was diluted, it is true, by an influx of newcomers into the second, post-1916, Sinn Féin, but a developmental thrust can still be discerned in Dáil rhetoric. The objects of the Dáil Loan, at least as formally expressed in April 1919, included the establishment of Counsellor services abroad to promote Irish trade, the development of sea fisheries, re-afforestation, and an industrial drive. If little was to happen in practice as war conditions enveloped the country, there is no intimation here of a desire to recreate an imagined world of rustic Celtic bliss, but rather of a determination to thrust the economy forward on a broad front.

Even seventy-five years later, the aspirations have a curiously contemporary ring. Many of the measures envisaged would only be activated after the passage of decades. So little had been done in the area of forestry, for example, that Seán MacBride could make an afforestation policy a central plank of Clann na Poblachta's programme thirty years later, and it would be another thirty years before the policy came to be generally accepted by the official mind. Fisheries remained so underdeveloped during the next half century that a special escape clause had to be inserted into the Treaty of Accession to the EEC in 1972 to provide some protection for a still infant industry.

Dáil declarations on the evils of over-taxation and depopulation appear particularly ironic in retrospect. Ireland was very lightly taxed in 1919 by later standards. But so was every other country. Ireland's population situation was much more distinctive than her taxation situation. The assumption that Ireland was seriously under-populated may appear naive to-day, when an increase of a half-million in the population of the Republic over the past twenty-five years is so frequently used as an explanation for our high levels of unemployment, taxation, emigration, dependency, and much else. When we have such difficulty coping with a population density only half that of Northern Ireland, or a quarter that of Italy, it is understandable that this once crucial criterion of national performance no longer features prominently in public discourse. It is a far cry from the thinking of 75 years ago, when it was a nationalist axiom that the unique fall in population from the mid-nineteenth century had been due to British misrule, and that as soon as that incubus was removed Irish population levels would soon reach Western European densities. Emigration was seen as both a symptom and a cause of economic and psychological malaise.

However simplistic this now seems to some, the fact does remain that the Dáil's aspiration was to bring Ireland broadly into line with Western Europe, whereas we have today persuaded ourselves that our deviance from European normalcy is itself normal – a classic case of an Irish solution to an Irish problem.

Exaggerated though some of the more ambitious projections of our economic potential may have been, a strong case can be made, not least in the light of our population record, that the economic performance of independent Ireland would fall, for much of the time, well below our potential.

Did the approach of the First Dáil contribute in any way to this? The issue is an important but elusive one, and must in the end remain a matter of opinion, depending on how one assesses various balances of probabilities. This is not to evade the issue, merely to warn of its complexity. If one holds, as I do – but many do not – that our marked tendency to imitate British precedent in a whole range of activities has tended, on balance, to inhibit rather than stimulate national development, then the example set by the Dáil in its own sphere may have been inimical to the national interest. Certainly, the incongruity of the Dáil adopting its procedures, and much of its tone, from Westminster precedent, even while it rejoiced in its abstention from Westminster, has often been noted. There was probably no realistic alternative in the immediate circumstances. The leaders had no time to meditate at leisure on the constitutional arrangements of other countries, or to think through the deeper implications of their own behaviour. They were virtually under siege. Their main objective was to assert Ireland's right to independence. They could not take a longer-term view when everything depended on the outcome of short-term confrontation. Conscious as they were of the importance of impressing a wider world with the dignity and decorum of their proceedings, and sensitive to the need to counter the image sedulously propagated by the unionist media, in England and Ireland, that the mere Irish were unfit for self-government, they could afford few procedural experiments.

It might also be argued that while the general style of the Dáil followed the Westminster model, nevertheless certain significant deviations did occur. The very fact that the Dáil adopted a broadly Westminster model partly through the mechanism of a written provisional constitution itself marks a notable departure from English precedent. The idea of a written constitution would take firm hold on the Irish political imagination, and in every subsequent Irish régime would come to constitute a quite significant difference in the political practice of the two jurisdictions. Ironically, another innovation that would lead to striking differences in political practice between the two countries was imposed by Westminster, in the form of the change in the electoral system from the British 'first past the post' style to proportional representation with multi-member constituencies, in the general election of 1921.

If the First Dáil did generally imitate the Westminster model, nevertheless it did not close off possibilities for revising procedures. Many options still remained open for its successors. In particular, the Westminster model cannot be considered independently of the Whitehall model. It was the adoption of the combination of the two, which was not consolidated until the Free State years, that really riveted the English style of government on the new state. The consequences for our administrative culture of the Ministers and Secretaries Act of 1924, which even today still holds Ministers responsible for every decision in their Department – a patently fictitious formulation which obliges civil servants to 'protect' their Minister – have become increasingly baneful in recent years.

The First Dáil cannot be held responsible for this. Its Ministers could not operate through a civil service in any normal sense. Some Dáil officials would indeed become distinguished civil servants, like Diarmuid O'Hegarty, Chief Clerk of the Dáil, a key if elusive figure in the creation of independent Ireland, who would become Secretary of the Executive Council from 1922 to 1932. Nevertheless, impressive though some achievements were, particularly in the area of local government and the courts, administration had to be largely conducted in an improvised manner. It was hard enough to keep track of what was happening in one's own Department, with activity disrupted by the harassing of key members, much less attempt coordination with other departments. It says something about the degree of administrative incoherence that an argument advanced for the publication of a regular Gazette, even during the more relaxed atmosphere of the Truce in 1921, was that it would help keep 'the various departments informed of each other's work'.[2]

If it was not civil servants who would exert decisive influence on the First Dáil, neither was it the members themselves. This was not due to any lack of commitment. Attendance was remarkably good in the circumstances. Suppressed by the British in September 1919 – the quality of British decision-making still showed touches worthy of North and Dartmouth[3] – the Dáil met on only twenty-one occasions over two and a half years. Many of the members were in jail or on the run for much of the time. The President himself, de Valera, felt it more important to be in America than in Ireland for more than half the life of the Dáil.

All this not only made it difficult for the Dáil to exert steady influence on the country, but made it impossible for the deputies to exert steady influence on the Cabinet. It even made it difficult for the Cabinet to exert collective influence on its strongest personalities, particularly Michael Collins. Some TDs felt so disturbed at their exclusion from decision-making by the small groups who revolved, often informally, around a relevant Minister or strong man, that they proposed the establishment of a formal committee system, through which ordinary backbenchers would be more actively involved in decision-making. Under strong driving from Collins and Griffith, conscious of the need for speed and secrecy, the Dáil rejected the proposal.

A committee system would find little favour with any Irish government until the very recent past. It has only recently begun to be tried in any coherent way, and still faces major problems if it is to function effectively. Insofar as a committee system has the potential to lead to more open government, it threatens to subvert the familiar coterie of Minister and senior civil servants that, most of the time, constitutes the decision-making axis around which Irish government revolves. Keeping backbenchers, as well as the public, as ignorant as possible, is a pre-requisite for the functioning of our system of government. It may be, depending on one's judgement of our political culture, that this is the best possible system. But most other western democracies operate through some variety of committee system, and there seems no objective reason why Ireland should not do the same. It is a necessary, if not sufficient, pre-requisite for more open government.

The ineffectuality of ordinary members meant that the First Dáil, like other representative assemblies, served mainly as the necessary fig leaf for the functioning of parliamentary democracy, by providing the veneer of representative legitimacy for decisions taken in practice by smaller groups. Parliaments do not, after all, actually decide very much, most of the time, in the real world, in Ireland or elsewhere. In a tightly organised party system like ours, probably essential to avoid the anarchy of innumerable factions, Dáil debates rarely make much difference to legislation. It is true that changes of opinion by Dáil deputies brought down John A Costello's government in 1951, de Valera's in 1954, Costello's again in 1957, Garret FitzGerald's and Charles Haughey's in 1982. In all these cases, however, the governments were relying on the support of independents, or of small parties, and the result depended on the decisions of a handful of TDs, not on the agonising of every deputy. The only occasions on which the whole body of TDs, acting in their individual capacity, decided major issues, were the vote on the Treaty in January 1922, and the subsequent election of Arthur Griffith instead of de Valera as President of the Dáil.

The real question is not whether parliament, or smaller groups, take the real decisions. It is, rather, which smaller groups enjoy decisive input into policy-making. Is it the cabinet, or senior civil servants, or parliamentary committees, or pressure groups, or some combination of these?

The power of pressure groups, benign or malign according to taste, is often held to be subversive of genuine parliamentary democracy. Although its role can be exaggerated, the Catholic hierarchy has been generally deemed the most influential pressure group in nationalist Ireland until very recently. It certainly exerted substantial influence on the Home Rule party, but it probably enjoyed less influence with the First Dáil than with most of its successors. Some individual members of the Dáil, like Seán T O'Kelly, had close connections with certain clergy, and the Dáil was of course conscious of the advantages of Church support. But it generally relied more on influencing the hierarchy through public opinion than on influencing public opinion through the hierarchy.

Education was the main area in which the Dáil, and de Valera in particular, took full cognizance of Church concerns.[4] Given that Pearse, so ritualistically revered in other circumstances, had declared that root and branch educational reform would be the first priority of an independent Ireland, de Valera's cabinet conspicuously failed to include a Minister for Education. As Cathal Brugha rather disingenuously put it, he 'thought President de Valera had some definite reason for not appointing a Minister of Education when he was constituting his Ministry'. Nevertheless, even the most fevered anti-Catholic imagination has to scale peaks of sectarian fervour to imagine the Dáil as the puppet of the bishops.

A Department of Irish, established belatedly several months after the formation of de Valera's cabinet, served as a short-term substitute for a Department of Education. In the judgement of Nollaig Ó Gadhra, the leading authority on the subject, however, it lacked imagination and energy. If nationalist protestations were to be taken at face value, the revival of the language was the greatest single cultural challenge facing the country. A high proportion of Dáil members were Gaelic Leaguers, including nearly all of de Valera's first cabinet. The proceedings on 21 January were conducted extensively through Irish. Cathal Brugha opened the Dáil in Irish with the acknowledgement that as there might be some present who did not understand the language, he would unfortunately have to say a few words in English. De Valera himself asserted in May that 'the official language of this Assembly is the Irish language'. But no serious attempt seems to have been undertaken to make Irish the real, as distinct from the official, language of the Dáil, or even of the Cabinet.

The speed with which the use of Irish declined alarmed some members. As early as 10 April 1919, Piaras Béaslaí indicated his forebodings by seeking a bilingual Cabinet and a bilingual Dáil, obviously feeling that this would mark a distinct improvement. In practice it was not only Labour that must wait, but the language that must wait, until the more urgent business of self-government was settled. But cultural and political objectives were not mutually exclusive. The abdication by the Dáil of responsibility for leading the revival – in which leading by example was the only way to lead at all – portended the fate of the language in the new régime. It was not with Free State governments, but with the First Dáil itself, that the slippage began. The Gaelic League failed to make its mark successfully on the political class when it might really have mattered.

Neither the Church nor the League constituted the main challenge for the Dáil. It was the military wing of the republican movement that exerted the most serious pressure. The relationship between the IRA, the IRB, and the Dáil would prove a tortuous one for several reasons.

The Sinn Féin manifesto for the 1918 election had, before it was mangled by the censor, claimed the right to use 'any and every means available to render impotent the power of England to hold Ireland in subjection by military force or otherwise'. However clear the general thrust of this, the phrase 'every means available' begged the question, 'available to whom?' In principle, to the Dáil. But the IRB, and the Volunteers/IRA, existed before the Dáil. There was a grim symbolism in the fact that the first ambush of the War of Independence occurred on the very day of the ceremonial opening of the Dáil, and without its authorisation. Supposing the military movement, or elements within it, refused to give allegiance to the Dáil? What then? Fundamental issues of principle would immediately arise. How would the elected representatives respond?[7]

In electoral terms, Sinn Féin had emerged from nowhere. But it had not come out of a political vacuum. Nationalist political culture, in contrast to that to the Unionist, provided a framework in which a democratic parliamentary process could flourish. But it did not guarantee it. Democracy is a much abused word, and a much manipulated concept. It cannot be equated, in a colonial situation, or within borders imposed by military diktat, with constitutionalism. They are related, but not identical, concepts. Democracy can only achieve its full flowering when the will of the people can be freely expressed.

The question of who constitutes 'the people' in a society riven by conflicting popular identities poses further difficult, if not insoluble, problems. But whoever the people may be, the mature expression of their will requires an apprenticeship in representative politics. The nationalist Irish had served that apprenticeship for over a century. The standard rhetoric of nineteenth-century nationalism revolved around the restoration of Grattan's Parliament, with the emphasis more on parliament than on Grattan. Daniel O'Connell, who did more than any single individual to create a popular political consciousness, directed the bulk of his formidable energies to influencing parliament. Parnell consolidated that achievement by fashioning a Parliamentary Party that could survive even his own cataclysmic fall, and by concentrating his campaign during the subsequent split on the struggle for parliamentary representation.

When Sinn Féin superseded the Home Rule Party in 1918, it did so not by rejecting representational politics, but by winning the election. Both parties were products of the same long-term process of modernisation. If Parnell's lieutenants, John Dillon, William

O'Brien, Tim Healy, Tim Harrington, Tim Sexton, and John Redmond, who came into parliament in the 1880s, lacked the Chief's charisma, they nevertheless constituted a respectable front bench. They represented the first generation of Catholic nationalists to form a political leadership cadre, emerging from a society where educational standards and literacy levels were rapidly rising, and from which much of the worst poverty was disappearing. Nationalist Ireland need no longer depend on charismatic figures for leadership.

The Home Rule generation was pushed aside in 1918. But it was pushed aside by a party that had a still deeper reservoir of talent. However few of its critics perceived it, the depth of leadership in Sinn Féin would enable it survive the loss of its leaders in traumatic circumstances. Three of its four most influential leaders in 1919, Collins, Griffith and Brugha, would die in 1922. The fourth, de Valera, would wander in the political wilderness between 1922 and 1927. It reflects the richness of the political resources of Sinn Féin that it was still those schooled in the party who provided stable government for the Free State for more than a generation after the Civil War. Very few new states of the twentieth century have been able to draw on such a reservoir of leadership ability at the time of independence.

The First Dáil was strikingly young compared with the Home Rule Party, with nearly 60% of members under the age of 40, and more than 20% under the age of 30. More striking still, it was vastly better educated than the country in general, and possibly better educated than the bulk of the early senior Civil Service, or several subsequent Dáils, with at least 60% boasting a secondary education, and nearly 30% university or professional education.[8] Even allowing for some double counting, and accepting that not all those who rose to high office were self-evidently superior beings, the 69 Sinn Féin members counted among their number two future Presidents of Ireland, three future Prime Ministers, at least ten future Ministers, two future General Secretaries of the Gaelic Athletic Association, the founder of the Educational Building Society, the founder of Waterford Glass and of the Irish Hospitals Sweepstake, a President of the Federation of Irish Industrialists, a Managing Director of the Abbey Theatre, and a President of the High Court, as well as several prominent military men and journalists.

In addition, where the Home Rule Party had become deeply immersed in local politics, the Sinn Féin deputies were selected disproportionately on their national rather than their local standing. 46% of them didn't even normally reside in their constituencies. The First Dáil was a parachutist's paradise. That would soon change. The political culture in general was far more localist than were the Sinn Féin deputies, many of whom not only transcended local interests, but cherished an austere sense of propriety in public affairs.

These were the members who faced the issue of where legitimate authority resided in the Republican movement, and what exactly their mandate meant. By one criterion, their views on the Treaty as recorded in January 1922, (which many observers would interpret as a verdict on the relative legitimacy of civilian and military rule) the survivors of the First Dáil divided almost evenly, 32 for the Treaty, 28 against.

The TDs wouldn't have necessarily seen it in quite that light, even in the context of the Treaty Debate, much less in the immediate aftermath of the 1918 election. It is tempting to think, from the perspective of 75 years later, particularly in the light of the Northern Ireland tragedy, that constitutional and insurrectionary were deemed to be mutually exclusive by the majority of the Irish people under the Union. There is an inclination to think of the parliamentarians and the military as representing conflicting ideological positions, with irreconcilable perspectives on the morality of physical force and on the sources of governmental legitimacy.

There were, at the extremes, contrasts along these lines. But most members were not at the extremes. There were conflicting impulses, as well as much overlap, confusion and inconsistency, not only between, but within, organisations, and not only between, but within, individuals. The organisations could accentuate these conflicts, but they reflected rather than created them. That was the main reason why all the most important ones – Dáil, IRA, IRB – split on the Treaty issue. It would be difficult to project responses to the Treaty from attitudes in the First Dáil. Collins was far less anxious than Brugha or de Valera to bring the IRA under civilian control in 1919, yet he died supporting the primacy of constitutional authority where Brugha died disputing it. As Kevin Nowlan has remarked, 'a number of the arguments advanced by the anti-Treaty Volunteers to justify their defiance of the Dáil Ministry must have sounded strangely familiar to some of their opponents who had to answer them'.[9]

Most of the nationalist people of Ireland seem to have blended, as far as we can tell, Tone and Emmet with O'Connell and Parnell into one tradition of resistance, distinguished more by tactical differences than by ideological cleavages, however ardently O'Connell preached the gospel of non-violence. The majority did not, again as far as we can tell, agonise over the morality of violence in a colonial situation, or deem government violence legitimate and insurrectionary violence illegitimate. Home Rule leaders generally denounced violence as impractical, not as immoral. Several accepted the morality of violence in as just a cause as Ireland's, but held the odds to be so heavily in favour of Britain's command of superior violence that insurrection would be futile.

There were those within the republican élite who developed more theoretical or abstract philosophies of insurrection. The tortuous theology of the Declaration of Independence in the opening session of the Dáil reflected rather than resolved the

153

ambiguities. According to this Declaration, the Dáil did not establish the Republic. It merely 'ratified' a Republic already in existence, a Republic proclaimed by the IRA on Easter Monday 1916. The drafters highlighted the incongruity by their immediate attempt to square the ideological circle by insisting the IRA was 'acting on behalf of the Irish people'.

But supposing the Irish people were to decide, for whatever reason, that they would not support the ratification of a Republic at a particular time? Who would then, in practice, decide? Were 'the Irish people' always right, or were they right only when their thinking happened to coincide with that of the IRA? The ambiguity did not have to be confronted quite so starkly during the First Dáil itself, although the introduction of an Oath of Allegiance in August 1919 sought to square the circle by demanding fealty from both the IRA and the Dáil to both the Republic and the Dáil, a cumbersome formulation reflecting the difficulty of reconciling two potentially conflicting allegiances.

There was likely to have been guerilla activity of some sort, Dáil or no Dáil, as the Volunteer action at Soloheadbeg intimated. It might have been suppressed rapidly and ruthlessly if Britain had not had to contend with the aura of legitimacy conferred in what we would today call the international community – mainly America and the Dominions, as well as in Britain itself – by the existence of the Dáil.

Suppose, however, that the guerilla war had succeeded in achieving a degree of independence with no Dáil in place? What sort of régime might then have emerged? Strong though the impulses towards democracy were in the political culture, there were also powerful impulses to the contrary. When a choice had to be made, there would always be those who would consider their authority to derive from an eternal historic right, not from the mandate of the moment. They were probably a minority. But they were activists. One could not preclude the possibility of a

Colonel's régime, a jackboot state, emerging for at least a period, as it has emerged in so many other new states in this century. It might have been superseded in due course. But by what process? By a mellowing of militaristic thinking? Or by internal coup, by bloody revolt, by Civil War potentially more savage than even the actual Civil War? This speculation must be kept within disciplined bounds. Nevertheless, it is necessary to speculate, if only to remind ourselves that there was nothing inevitable about the course of events.

The establishment of the First Dáil as the legitimate representative of the democratically expressed wishes of the Irish people (or the Irish nationalist people, depending on perspective), did not guarantee that democracy would triumph against either British militarism in Ireland or Irish militarism. As long as the British insisted on holding Ireland by violence, then violence would play a major role in settling the issues at conflict. So it did, firstly by imposing the precise line of partition in the Government of Ireland Act of 1920, which remains to this day the most spectacular example that violence does pay in Anglo-Irish relations. There can, of course, be genuine differences of opinion about the legitimacy of a separate Unionist jurisdiction in principle, depending on various views about the identities to which self-determination should apply. But there can be no legitimate difference of opinion – on the basis of any principle of self-government – on the legitimacy of the precise line of partition. Even Lloyd George, never one to miss a negotiating point, conceded as much on the issue of Fermanagh and Tyrone. The actual line stands as a stark reminder of the triumph of violence over representational reason. It was violence too that induced the subsequent shift in the British position between the terms of the Government of Ireland Act and the vastly more concessionary terms of the Treaty, less than a year later.

How then does one strike a balanced conclusion on the significance of the First Dáil? The circumstances in which it found itself obliged to operate were so peculiar that it would be unhistorical to venture too dogmatic a verdict. It could be said, rather brusquely, that its most important achievements were simply to have come into existence in the first place, and then to have survived. It found itself trying to establish democratic government in the face of bitter opposition from a powerful enemy, committed to physical force unionism, which waged a cynical campaign of violence and vituperation against elected representatives.

It was important that the Treaty negotiations did not occur with the IRA, but with the Dáil. In the internal conflict that would tear Sinn Féin apart after the Treaty, only the existence of the Dáil provided a forum in which public opinion could be heard. Even the limited experience of the First Dáil may have allowed some who might otherwise have been able to think of themselves only as rebels – above all, Collins – to begin conceiving of themselves as democrats also.

The First Dáil managed to keep most of the options for future national development, at least in the South, open. Packed with strong personalities, and potentially riven by personal and ideological rivalries, it succeeded in conducting its affairs in a responsible manner. If it had its fair share of illusion, opportunism and calculation, it had more than its fair share of courage, idealism and determination. In many respects what was significant about the Dáil was the manner in which it won and retained the allegiance of a people of whose more mundane concerns it was, in composition and disposition, often unrepresentative.

If Ireland counts among the few new states of the time to have sustained democratic stability, much of the credit should be given to the First Dáil, which played a central role, in almost impossible circumstances, in establishing the institutions, at however embryonic a stage, and fostering the attitudes, that would ensure that the centre did hold.

Notes

1. Dáil Éireann, Minutes of Proceedings of the First Parliament of he Republic of Ireland 1919-1921 (Dublin, n.d.). For a judicious assessment see DS Johnson, *'The Belfast Boycott, 1920-1922'*, in JM Goldstrom and LA Clarkson (eds.), *Irish population, economy, and society: essays in honour of the late KH Connell* (Oxford, 1981), pp. 287-308. For de Valera's more malleable personal attitude during 1921 see John Bowman, *De Valera and the Ulster Question 1917-1973* (Oxford 1982), pp. 44ff.

2. For an admirable analysis of the calibre of British decision-making in London and Dublin see E O'Halpin, *The decline of the Union: British government in Ireland 1892-1920* (Dublin, 1987), pp. 157-213.

3. Gerard O'Brien, *'The record of the First Dáil debates'*, Irish Historical Studies, XXVIII, III (May 1993), p. 308.

4. Dáil Éireann, 27 October, 1919, p. 163. For the wider educational context see Séamas O' Buachalla, *Education Policy in Twentieth-Century Ireland* (Dublin 1988), pp. 54-5. For the more general church/state context see D W Miller, *Church, state and nation in Ireland 1898-1921* (Pittsburgh, 1973), Chs XIX, XX, and Dermot Keogh, *The Vatican, the Bishops and Irish politics 1919-39* (Cambridge, 1986), Ch. 2.

5. For an example of juvenile anti-Catholicism in Dublin Castle, see O'Halpin, pp. 184-5, 204.

6. See N Ó Gadhra, *An Chéad Dáil Éireann (1919-1921) agus an Ghaeilge* (BAC, 1989), pp. 203-05. See also P MacAonghusa, *Ar Son na Gaeilge: Conradh na Gaeilge 1893-1993* (BAC, 1993), p. 166.

7. The seminal study stimulating reflections of this type is Brian Farrell, *The founding of Dáil Éireann: parliament and nation building* (Dublin, 1971).

8. J L McCracken, *Representative government in Ireland. A study of Dáil Éireann 1919-48* (London, 1958), Chs 2 and 3, pioneered the structural study of the First Dáil.

9. K B Nowlan, *'Dáil Éireann and the army: unity and division (1919-1921)'*, in TD Williams (ed), *The Irish struggle 1916-1926* (London, 1966), p. 77.

APPENDICES

Appendix 1:
(re. Essay Number 3 by John Coakley)
A note on the results of the General Election of 1918.

Appendix 2:
(re: Essay Number 5 by Brian Farrell)
2a: The Constitution of Dáil Éireann
2b: The Democratic Programme of the First Dáil
2c: The Johnson Draft of the Democratic Programme
2d: Declaration of Independence
2e: Message to the Free Nations of the World
2f: Check-list of Dáil Decrees 1919 -1922

APPENDIX 1

A NOTE ON THE RESULTS OF
THE GENERAL ELECTION OF 1918

Electorate. Data on the electorate, area and population of each constituency are available in *Return Showing, for each Parliamentary Constituency in the United Kingdom, the Numbers of Parliamentary and Local Electors on the First Register compiled under the Representation of the People Act, 1918*, pp. 20-23, in *British Parliamentary Papers*, 1918, vol. XIX (138).

Votes. Unlike other British elections, the results of the election of 1918 were never officially published, and the manuscript returns kept in the parliamentary archives do not report the numbers of votes cast (letter from Dr Chris Pond, Public Information Office, House of Commons, 17 May 1994). FWS Craig, compiler of the definitive collection of British election statistics covering this period, *British Parliamentary Election Statistics 1918-1968* (Glasgow: Political Reference Publications, 1968), used the 1922 edition of *Debrett's Illustrated House of Commons and Judicial Bench* as the source for this election, citing (p. xi) the editors' claim to have checked their tabulations with the returning officers in each constituency, and this has in general been followed in Brian M Walker (ed.) *Parliamentary Election Results in Ireland, 1801-1922* (Dublin: Royal Irish Academy, 1978). A check against other similar sources, including *Dod's Parliamentary Companion, 1920*, *Whitaker's Almanac, 1919* and *Thom's Directory, 1919*, and with the yearbooks of the major political parties, including *The Constitutional Year Book, 1919*, *The Labour Year Book 1919* and *The Liberal Year Book for 1926* confirms almost all of these, if certain obvious misprints are disregarded. However, in four cases (the Sinn Féin vote in Mid Armagh, Belfast Victoria and Donegal East, and the Nationalist vote in Down East) all of these sources except the *Liberal Year Book* agree on a different figure from that in *Debrett's*, while in a fifth, the Nationalist vote in Roscommon South, all of these sources except *Thom's Directory* agree on a different figure. Contemporary newspaper reports (the *Freeman's Journal*, the *Irish Times*, the (Dublin) *Daily Express*, the *Cork Examiner*, the *Irish News*, the *Belfast Telegraph*, the *Belfast Newsletter* and the *Northern Whig*, 30 December 1918) in general confirm the accuracy of this consensus in the case of the first four of these figures, but disagree on the fifth. A local newspaper, the *Roscommon Herald*, 4 January 1919, provides a detailed and internally consistent account of the returning officer's announcement, which confirms the accuracy of the newspapers (except the *Freeman's Journal*) rather than that of the yearbooks.

Party affiliations. The sources mentioned above agree on almost all of these; in doubtful cases, the source closest politically to the attributed party label has been relied on (for example, five candidates in Belfast described variously as 'Labour Representation Committee' and 'Independent Labour' have been designated here as 'Labour', following the *Labour Year Book*). Unionists include three candidates of the Ulster Unionist Labour Association in Belfast (all elected; 30,304 votes). In the territorial constituencies 'others' include Labour (5 candidates, all in Belfast;12,823 votes), and eight independent candidates, of whom four were of a nationalist orientation (6,217 votes), three of a unionist orientation (8,738 votes) and one indeterminate (436 votes).

Computation of results. The accompanying table reports the results for the territories of the two contemporary states, the Republic of Ireland and Northern Ireland. In Cork City each elector had two votes; following the procedure adopted in FWS Craig, *British Parliamentary Election Statistics 1918-1968*, p. xi, each vote in this constituency has been counted as half a vote (the actual votes were Sinn Féin 41,307, Nationalists 14,642 and Unionists 4,773). The results also need to be interpreted in the light of the comments in the two following notes. The university constituency results have been reported separately. Dublin University returned two members, but these were elected in 1918 by the single transferable vote.

The Nationalist-Sinn Féin pact. Voting in the eight constituencies covered by the Nationalist-Sinn Féin pact was as follows (successful candidates' votes bolded; in a ninth constituency, Fermanagh North, a plebiscite of 5,763 nationalist voters had decided by a majority of 3,737 to 2,026, or 64.8%, to put forward a Sinn Féin candidate only; *Northern Whig*, 3 December 1918):

Constituency	Allocation Sinn Féin	Nationalist	Unionist
Down South*	33	**8,756**	5,573
Donegal East	40	**7,596**	4,797
Tyrone Northeast	56	**11,605**	6,681
Armagh South	79	**4,345**	-
Down East	3,876	4,312	**6,007**
Fermanagh South	**6,673**	132	4,524
Londonderry City	**7,335**	120	7,020
Tyrone Northwest	**10,442**	-	7,696

*an independent candidate won 436 votes in Down South

Unopposed returns. Sinn Féin candidates were returned unopposed in the following 25 constituencies: all seven constituencies in Cork county, all four constituencies in Kerry, two of the four Tipperary constituencies, both of the constituencies in the counties of Cavan and Clare, one of the four constituencies in Galway and Mayo, one of the two in Kilkenny, Limerick and Roscommon, the single-constituency counties of Carlow and King's County, and Limerick City.

Party support. The considerable number of unopposed returns has permitted sharply conflicting estimates of Sinn Féin strength in 1918. The most negative interpretation treats all non-voters in contested constituencies as non-Sinn Féin supporters, or even expresses the Sinn Féin vote as a percentage of the total electorate (see Sir James O'Connor, *History of Ireland 1798-1924*, vol. 2, London, Edward Arnold, 1926, p. 293; estimates A and B below). The most positive interpretation treats all electors in constituencies in which a Sinn Féin candidate was returned unopposed as Sinn Féin voters (see Eamon De Valera, *The Foundation of the Republic of Ireland in the Votes of the People: Results of the General Election of December 1918—A National Plebiscite Held under British Law and British Supervision*, New York, n.p, n.d.; estimate E below). Sinn Féin strength may be estimated more accurately by making assumptions about its probable minimum support in uncontested constituencies. If we assume that in the 25 uncontested constituencies the turnout was the same as that in the contested constituencies in the 26 counties (68.0%), and that party support was at the same level (for instance, Sinn Féin winning 65.3%), then we can estimate that at least 44.4% (65.3% of 68.0%) of the 474,778 electors in the uncontested constituencies would have supported Sinn Féin had they had the opportunity of doing so (this is probably an underestimate of Sinn Féin support). Because of the importance of this debate for the issue of the electorate's 'endorsement' of the republican position, these four estimates are reported below, together with the actual result (C). These are:

A - party vote as percentage of total
electorate
B - party vote as percentage of electorate
in contested constituencies
C - party vote as percentage of total valid
poll (the formal result)

D - As C, but including an estimate for
party support in uncontested
constituencies (best estimate of
minimum Sinn Féin support)
E - as D, but assuming all electors in
uncontested Sinn Féin constituencies
were Sinn Féin voters.

Party	A	B	C	D	E
Sinn Féin	24.6	32.7	47.0	51.5	64.0
Nationalists	14.9	19.8	21.7	22.9	19.3
Unionists	11.4	15.1	28.4	23.3	14.8
Others	1.5	1.9	2.8	2.3	1.9
Non-voters	47.6	30.5	-	-	-

RESULTS OF GENERAL ELECTION OF 1918, IRELAND

	Southern Ireland Number	%	Northern Ireland Number	%	All Ireland Number	%
Electorate						
Total	1,371,911	100.0	554,363	100.0	1,926,274	100.0
women	*485,426*	*35.4*	*210,609*	*38.0*	*696,035*	*36.1*
military personnel	*64,395*	*4.7*	*45,016*	*8.1*	*109,411*	*5.7*
business votes	*8,396*	*0.6*	*7,115*	*1.3*	*15,511*	*0.8*
Votes						
Total	610,056	100.0	398,608	100.0	1,008,664	100.0
Sinn Féin	398,619	65.3	75,922	19.0	474,541	47.0
Unionists	32,928	5.4	253,899	63.7	286,827	28.4
Nationalists	174,742	28.6	44,341	11.1	219,083	21.7
Others	3,768	0.6	24,446	6.1	28,214	2.8
Candidates						
Total	130	100.0	74	100.0	204	100.0
Sinn Féin	72	55.4	28	37.8	100	49.0
Unionists	9	6.9	27	36.5	36	17.6
Nationalists	46	35.4	9	12.2	55	27.0
Others	3	2.3	10	13.5	13	6.4
Seats						
Total	72	100.0	29	100.0	101	100.0
Sinn Féin	69	95.8	3	10.3	72	71.3
Unionists	1	1.4	22	75.9	23	22.8
Nationalists	2	2.8	4	13.8	6	5.9
Others	0	0.0	0	0.0	0	0.0
Universities						
Electorate	8,360	100.0	2,039	100.0	10,399	100.0
women	*504*	*6.0*	*141*	*6.9*	*645*	*6.2*
Votes	5,411	100.0	1,605	100.0	7,016	100.0
Sinn Féin	1,644	30.4	118	7.4	1,762	25.1
Unionists	1,904	35.2	1,487	92.6	3,391	48.3
Nationalists	1,070	19.8	0	0.0	1,070	15.3
Others	793	14.7	0	0.0	793	11.3

Note: the data on women, military and business voters are included in the 'total' figure for the electorate. There were eight candidates for the university seats (two Unionists, two Nationalists, one Sinn Féin in the north). Four university members were elected (one Unionist, one independent unionist and one Sinn Féin in the South, one Unionist in the North). The total number of candidates was slightly less than the number reported here due to double (or even multiple) candidacies.

APPENDIX 2a
THE CONSTITUTION OF DÁIL ÉIREANN

Article 1
All legislative powers shall be vested in Dáil Éireann, composed of Deputies, elected by the Irish people from the existing Irish Parliamentary constituencies.

Article 2
(a) All executive powers shall be vested in the members, for the time being, of the Ministry.

(b) The Ministry shall consist of a President of the Ministry, elected by Dáil Éireann and four Executive officers, viz:
A Secretary of Finance
A Secretary of Home Affairs
A Secretary of Foreign Affairs
A Secretary of National Defence
each of whom the President shall nominate and have the power to dismiss.

(c) Every member of the Ministry shall be a member of Dáil Éireann and shall at all times be responsible to the Dáil.

(d) At the first meeting of Dáil Éireann after their nomination by the President, the names of the Executive Officers shall be separately submitted to Dáil Éireann for approval.

(e) The appointment of the President shall date from his election, and the appointment of each Executive Officer from the date of the approval by the Dáil of his nomination.

(f) The Ministry or any members thereof may at any time be removed by vote of the Dáil upon motion for that specific purpose, provided that at least seven days notice in writing of that motion shall have been given.

Article 3
A Chairman elected annually by the Dáil, and in his absence a Deputy Chairman so elected, shall preside at all meetings of Dáil Éireann. Only members of the Dáil shall be eligible for these offices. In case of the
absence of the Chairman and Deputy Chairman the Dáil shall fill the
vacancies or elect a temporary Chairman.

Article 4
All monies required by the Ministry shall be obtained on vote of the Dáil. The Ministry shall be responsible to the Dáil for all monies so obtained, and shall present properly audited accounts for the expenditure of the same—twice yearly—in the months of May and November. The audit shall be conducted by an Auditor or Auditors appointed by the Dáil. No member of the Dáil shall be eligible for such appointment.

Article 5
This Constitution is provisional and is liable to alteration upon seven days written notice of motion for that specific purpose.

APPENDIX 2b

THE DEMOCRATIC PROGRAMME OF THE FIRST DÁIL

We declare in the words of the Irish Republican Proclamation the right of the people of Ireland to the ownership of Ireland, and to the unfettered control of Irish destinies to be indefeasible, and in the language of our first President, Pádraig MacPhiarais, we declare that the Nation's sovereignty extends not only to all men and women of the Nation, but to all its material possessions; the Nation's soil and all its resources, all the wealth and all the wealth-producing processes within the Nation, and with him we reaffirm that all rights to private property must be subordinated to the public right and welfare.

We declare that we desire our country to be ruled in accordance with the principles of Liberty, Equality and Justice for all, which alone can secure permanence of Government in the willing adhesion of the people.

We affirm the duty of every man and woman to give allegiance and service to the Commonwealth, and declare it is the duty of the Nation to assure that every citizen shall have opportunity to spend his or her strength and faculties in the service of the people. In return for willing service, we, in the name of the Republic, declare the right of every citizen to an adequate share of the produce of the Nation's labour.

It shall be the first duty of the Government of the Republic to make provision for the physical, mental and spiritual well-being of the children, to secure that no child shall suffer hunger or cold from lack of food, clothing, or shelter, but that all shall be provided with the means and facilities requisite for their proper education and training as Citizens of a Free and Gaelic Ireland.

The Irish Republic fully realises the necessity of abolishing the present odious, degrading and foreign Poor Law System, substituting therefor a sympathetic native scheme for the care of the Nation's aged and infirm, who shall not be regarded as a burden, but rather entitled to the Nation's gratitude and consideration. Likewise it shall be the duty of the Republic to take such measures as will safeguard the health of the people and ensure the physical as well as the moral well-being of the Nation .

It shall be our duty to promote the development of the Nation's resources, to increase the productivity of its soil, to exploit its mineral deposits, peat bogs, and fisheries, its waterways and harbours, in the interests and for the benefit of the Irish People.

It shall be the duty of the Republic to adopt all measures necessary for the recreation and invigoration of our industries, and to ensure their being developed on the most beneficial and progressive co-operative and industrial lines. With the adoption of an extensive Irish Consular Service, trade with foreign Nations shall be revived on terms of mutual advantage and good will, and while undertaking the organisation of the Nation's trade, import and export, it shall be the duty of the Republic to prevent the shipment from Ireland of food and other necessaries until the wants of the Irish people are fully satisfied and the future provided for.

It shall devolve upon the national Government to seek co-operation of the Governments of other countries in determining a standard of social and Industrial Legislation with a view to a general and lasting improvement in the conditions under which the working classes live and labour.

APPENDIX 2c

THE JOHNSON DRAFT OF THE DEMOCRATIC PROGRAMME

Repeating in the words of the Proclamation of the Provisional Government of the Irish Republic 'We declare the right of the people of Ireland to the ownership of Ireland and to the unfettered control of Irish destinies to be indefeasible'.

And further in the opinion of its President, P. H. Pearse, we declare that the nation's sovereignty extends not only to all the men and women of the nation but to all the material possessions of the nation: the nation's soil and all its resources, all wealth and all wealth-producing processes within the nation. In other words no private right to property is good against the public right of the nation (*Sovereign People*, by Pádraig H. Pearse, 31/3/1916.)

We declare further that as the nation in the exercise of its sovereignty may entrust its soil and its resources, its wealth and wealth-producing processes to the care and charge of any of its citizens, to use and exploit for the nation's enrichment, on such terms and on such conditions as may be determined by the whole people, so the nation must ever retain the right and the power to resume possession of such soil or such wealth whenever the trust is abused or the trustee fails to give faithful service.

In the same manner as we affirm that the duty of every man and woman is to give allegiance and service to the commonwealth, so we declare it as the duty of the nation to ensure that every citizen shall have the opportunity for spending his or her strength and faculties in the labour of wealth-producing or the service of the people. In return for willing service in the name of the Republic we declare the right of the nation's citizens to an adequate share of the produce of the nation's labour.

The Irish Republic shall always count its wealth and prosperity by the measure of health and happiness of its citizens. It shall, therefore, be the first duty of the Government of the Republic to make provision for the physical, mental and spiritual well-being of the children, to ensure that no child shall endure hunger or cold from lack of food, clothing or shelter, that all shall be provided with ample means and facilities requisite for the education and training of free citizens of a free Gaelic nation. A condition precedent to such education is to encourage by every reasonable means the most capable, sympathetic men and women to devote their talents to the education of the young.

To promote the development of its resources, to increase the productivity of its soil, to exploit its mineral deposits, peat bogs, fisheries, waterways and harbours in the interest of and for the benefit of the Irish people, the nation, exercising its right of sovereignty, shall deem it to be a duty to organise and direct into fruitful contact the labour of men with the land and raw materials and machinery and industry.

Wherever the land, the mineral deposits and other forms of the production of wealth are wrongly used or withheld from use to the detriment of the Republic, then the nation shall resume possession without compensation.

In the sphere of overseas commerce the Republican Government to safeguard the interests of the nation shall itself undertake the organisation of the import and export of merchandise so as to prevent the shipment from Ireland of food and other necessities until the wants of the Irish people are fully satisfied and the future provided for and to obviate the waste of life and labour which competitive commerce involves and the risk of destroying Irish productive enterprises.

It shall be the purpose of the Government to encourage the organisation of people into trade unions and co-operative societies with a view to the control and administration of the industries by the workers engaged in the industries. It shall also devolve upon the National Government to seek the co-operation of the governments of other nations in determining a standard of social and industrial legislation with a view to general improvement in the conditions under which the working classes live and labour.

Finally, the Republic will aim at the elimination of the class in society which lives upon the wealth produced by the workers of the nation but gives no useful service in return, and in the process of accomplishment will bring freedom to all who have hitherto been caught in the toils of economic servitude.

APPENDIX 2d

DECLARATION OF INDEPENDENCE

Whereas the Irish people is by right a free people:

And Whereas for seven hundred years the Irish people has never ceased to repudiate and has repeatedly protested in arms against foreign usurpation:

And Whereas English rule in this country is, and always has been, based upon force and fraud and maintained by military occupation against the declared will of the people:

And Whereas the Irish Republic was proclaimed in Dublin on Easter Monday, 1916, by the Irish Republican Army acting on behalf of the Irish people:

And Whereas the Irish people is resolved to secure and maintain its complete independence in order to promote the common weal, to re-establish justice, to provide for future defence, to insure peace at home and goodwill with all nations and to constitute a national policy based upon the people's will with equal right and equal opportunity for every citizen:

And Whereas at the threshold of a new era in history the Irish electorate has in the General Election of December, 1918, seized the first occasion to declare by an overwhelming majority its firm allegiance to the Irish Republic:

Now, therefore, we, the elected Representatives of the ancient Irish people in National Parliament assembled, do, in the name of the Irish nation, ratify the establishment of the Irish Republic and pledge ourselves and our people to make this declaration effective by every means at our command:

We ordain that the elected Representatives of the Irish people alone have power to make laws binding on the people of Ireland, and that the Irish Parliament is the only Parliament to which that people will give its allegiance:

We solemnly declare foreign government in Ireland to be an invasion of our national right which we will never tolerate, and we demand the evacuation of our country by the English Garrison:

We claim for our national independence the recognition and support of every free nation in the world, and we proclaim that independence to be a condition precedent to international peace hereafter:

In the name of the Irish people we humbly commit our destiny to Almighty God who gave our fathers the courage and determination to persevere through long centuries of a ruthless tyranny, and strong in the justice of the cause which they have handed down to us, we ask His divine blessing on this the last stage of the struggle we have pledged ourselves to carry through to Freedom.

APPENDIX 2e

MESSAGE TO THE FREE NATIONS OF THE WORLD

To the Nations of the World ! Greeting.

The Nation of Ireland having proclaimed her national independence, calls through her elected representatives in Parliament assembled in the Irish Capital on January 21st, 1919, upon every free nation to support the Irish Republic by recognising Ireland's national status and her right to its vindication at the Peace Congress.

Nationally, the race, the language, the customs and traditions of Ireland are radically distinct from the English. Ireland is one of the most ancient nations in Europe, and she has preserved her national integrity, vigorous and intact, through seven centuries of foreign oppression: she has never relinquished her national rights, and throughout the long era of English usurpation she has in every generation defiantly proclaimed her inalienable right of nationhood down to her last glorious resort to arms in 1916.

Internationally, Ireland is the gateway of the Atlantic. Ireland is the last outpost of Europe towards the West: Ireland is the point upon which great trade routes between East and West converge: her independence is demanded by the Freedom of the Seas: her great harbours must be open to all nations, instead of being the monopoly of England. To-day these harbours are empty and idle solely because English policy is determined to retain Ireland as a barren bulwark for English aggrandisement, and the unique geographical position of this island, far from being a benefit and safeguard to Europe and America, is subjected to the purposes of England's policy of world domination.

Ireland to-day reasserts her historic nationhood the more confidently before the new world emerging from the War, because she believes in freedom and justice as the fundamental principles of international law, because she believes in a frank co-operation between the peoples for equal rights against the vested privileges of ancient tyrannies, because the permanent peace of Europe can never be secured by perpetuating military dominion for the profit of empire but only by establishing the control of government in every land upon the basis of the free will of a free people, and the existing state of war, between Ireland and England, can never be ended until Ireland is definitely evacuated by the armed forces of England.

For these among other reasons, Ireland — resolutely and irrevocably determined at the dawn of the promised era of self-determination and liberty that she will suffer foreign dominion no longer — calls upon every free nation to uphold her national claim to complete Independence as an Irish Republic against the arrogant pretentions of England founded in fraud and sustained only by an overwhelming military occupation, and demands to be confronted publicly with England at the Congress of the Nations, in order that the civilised world having judged between English wrong and Irish right may guarantee to Ireland its permanent support for the maintenance of her national independence.

APPENDIX 2f

CHECK-LIST OF DÁIL DECREES, 1919-1922

File No.	Title of Decree	Session	No. of Decree
1.	Declaration of Independence	21st January, 1919	1/1919
2.	Democratic Programme	21st January, 1919	2/1919
3.	Loan Issue	10th April, 1919	3/1919
4.	Establishment of Consular Services	18th June, 1919	4/1919
5.	Provision of Land	18th June, 1919	5/1919
6.	Afforestation	18th June, 1919	6/1919
7.	Fisheries	18th June, 1919	7/1919
8.	National Arbitration Courts	18th June, 1919	8/1919
9.	National Civil Service	18th June, 1919	9/1919
10.	Industrial Commission of Inquiry	18th June, 1919	10/1919
11.	Housing	19th June, 1919	11/1919
12.	Loan Issue in America	20th August, 1919	12/1919
13.	Oath of Allegiance	20th August, 1919	13/1919
14.	Election Campaign for the Presidency of U.S.A.	29th June, 1920	1/ 1920
15.	Consuls and Diplomatic Agents	29th June, 1920	2/1920
16.	Ambassador to Washington	29th June, 1920	3/1920
17.	Diplomatic Mission	29th June, 1920	4/1920
18.	Courts of Justice and Equity	29th June, 1920	5/1920
19.	Claims to Land	29th June, 1920	6/1920
20.	Income Tax	29th June, 1920	7/1920
21.	Closing of Loan Issue	29th June, 1920	8/1920
22.	Commission re Local Administration	29th June, 1920	9/1920
23.	Import and Export Company	29th June, 1920	10/1920
24.	Imposition of Political or Religious Tests	6th August, 1920	11/1920
25.	Organised Opposition to the Republic	6th August, 1920	12/1920
26.	Increase of Rent	6th August, 1920	13/1920
27.	Emigration from Ireland	6th August, 1920	14/1920
28.	Severance of connection with Local Government Board	17th September, 1920	15/1920
29.	Terms of Reference of Commission on Organised Opposition to the Republic	17th September, 1920	16/1920
30.	Non-recognition of Hostile Legislation	17th September, 1920	17/1920
31.	National Economic Council	17th September, 1920	18/1920
32.	National Land Commission	17th September, 1920	19/1920
33.	Local Government Code of Laws	25th January, 1921	1/1921
34.	Prohibition of Census	11th March, 1921	2/1921
35.	Increase of Rent and Mortgage Interest	11th March, 1921	3/1921
36.	Exclusion of British Goods	11th March, 1921	4/1921
36a.	Exclusion of British Goods (Supplemental)	10th May, 1921	5/1921
37.	Registration of Births, Marriages and Deaths	Ist March, 1922	1/1922
38.	Ard Fheis Agreement	2nd March, 1922	2/1922
39.	General Election	20th May, 1922	3/1922

File No.	Title of Decree	Session	No. of Decree
40.	Membership of Local Authorities	8th June, 1922	4/1922
41.	Limerick Night Watchmen	8th June, 1922	5/1922
42.	County Scheme—Temporary Provisions	8th June, 1922	6/1922
43.	Secondary Education	8th June, 1922	7/1922
44.	Workman's Compensation (War Addition) Extension	8th June, 1922	8/1922